The Successful Coffee House

22-Day Action Plan to Create a Relevant and Profitable Business

DAVID J. MORRIS and **CHRIS HEYER**
Co-CEOs, Dillanos Coffee Roasters

with **Lon LaFlamme**

"The definitive industry guide for the retail specialty coffee business."

Sarah Allen
Editor, Barista Magazine

For more information contact:
PRESS 22 Publishers
800-234-5282

ISBN Hardcover: 978-0-692-44187-9

Contents

Acknowledgements and Special Thanks

There are so many specialty coffee industry leaders to thank, we simply can't list all who have influenced our lives in starting and growing Dillanos Coffee Roasters to the international, award-winning status it has today. That would be a separate book by itself.

First of all, we would like to recognize the significant contributions and guidance for this book provided by Dillanos' customer business development and marketing leader Lon LaFlamme.

The next person we would like to thank is Lauren Lyddon. Her unwavering commitment to finishing this book was extraordinary. Her countless hours spent editing will not soon be forgotten. We would also like to acknowledge the support and insight from Sarah Allen, editor of Barista magazine, who provided a critical review of every word written in this book, Shaun Nestor for his perspective on social media, and Jan Weigel, publisher and president of Fresh Cup magazine. We would also like to thank our friends Jeff Woods, Keith Hayward, and

David and Marni Heilbrunn for their numerous contributions. We make references throughout this book to Joe Lloyd of Durango Joes in Durango, Colorado, Gregory Zamfotis, founder of Gregory's Coffee house chain in Manhattan, New York, Bryan Reynolds, founder of Anthem Coffee & Tea in Puyallup, Washington, Wes Herman, founder of Woods Coffee in Bellingham, Washington, Patrick Burns of Palace Coffee Company in Amarillo, Texas, Michael Maler of Espresso Cielo in Palm Springs, California, Tom Palm of Design & Layout Services in Minneapolis, Minnesota, Shane Murphy of Java Espress in Idaho Falls, Idaho, Melissa and Ray Vandervalk of Red Leaf Organic Coffee in Kelso, Washington, and Ali Ghambari and Laila Ghambari of Cherry Street Coffee, Andrew Milstead of Milstead Coffee, and David Schomer of Espresso Vivace, all of Seattle, Washington.

Finally, we genuinely thank Chris Buck of Dillanos Coffee Roasters for his "Monday Morning Playbook" contribution, Dillanos Director of Coffee, Phil Beattie, and Dillanos business development representatives Kristen Hardcastle and Mandy Startzman for coffee and barista training insights that heavily contributed to the integrity of this handbook for success.

Our final words of thanks go out to every other staff member of Dillanos who lives our mission statement every day.

1) Help People.
2) Make Friends.
3) Have Fun.

A Note To The Reader
by Sarah Allen

One of the best things about the specialty coffee community is its warm embrace of the dreamer. Anything and everything is possible within this kinship of creativity, entrepreneurship, and craft. Small business owners abound, and with them and for them come associations, advisors, and resources. Here's how that "best thing," however, can be dangerous: Just as the coffee community celebrates visionaries striving to realize their coffee aspirations as café owners, roasters, or professional baristas, it unwittingly makes room for unfit counsel. Anyone can make their dreams come true in coffee, sure, but anyone can claim to be an expert with awesome advice for sale as well. I can't tell you how many times I've fielded phone calls from woeful would-be café owners who'd just spent truckloads of money on workshops, or certification programs promising the secrets to success, only to come out the other end with little to show for their efforts and cash.

Coffee professionals are busy people. They don't have time to navigate the murky waters of information and consultants out there. Can't someone just give them the real deal?

I'm here to say you've found it. Rule of thumb for new coffee business owners: Find experts who don't just say they're experts. Find the ones with the background to prove it. David J. Morris and Chris Heyer are well into their third decade of successful coffee business operations with Dillanos Coffee Roasters in Washington. They'll be the first to tell you there's no one key to coffee victory—it's a combination of strong business practices, capable people, and high standards for quality. Those are the three legs upon which Dillanos stands; it's what has positioned the Northwest company to win accolades not just in the coffee world—most prestigiously, being named USA Roaster of the Year by Roast Magazine in 2011—but in the business community as well. The Seattle-based South Sound Business Examiner named Dillanos the Best Place to Work not once, but twice in recent years.

My job as editor of Barista Magazine is to research and read, to review systems, and predict trends. For the past ten years, I've talked to coffee professionals from around the world almost every day. I think I have a pretty good idea about where the most reliable, not to mention useful, information comes from. The coffee business owners I turn to again and again as resources are the ones who have the chops to make almost any business work. What makes them so successful in this industry is combining that business know-how with a profound appreciation for, and curiosity about, the coffee business specifically. They want to know about all aspects of coffee, from the people who make it, to those who drink it, to the culture around it, to the product itself.

You might think a company that's found such success as Dillanos clearly has would play it close to the vest. Then, I'd say, you need to get to know these guys. That's just not how they do things. With success came Chris and David's desire to share with the coffee world around them. They want to see this industry thrive for everyone's benefit, and if that means sharing the formula, then they gladly will. In fact, here it is. If I was going to open a café, this is the book I would read. David and Chris present complicated information in a logical way. They've put together a strategy and timeline that can work in any environment. They've anticipated the roadblocks, both tangible and mental, as you wrap your head around the business of coffee, and they offer solutions and guidance that works.

I'm honored to introduce you to one of the most trusted resources I can recommend: this book you hold in your hands. Read it and then read it again. Fold down the pages. Highlight passages. Keep it close at hand because you'll want to refer to it again and again. Welcome to the coffee world. There's so much excitement in store for you.

Sarah Allen
Editor
Barista Magazine

Foreward

Let me jump right into why I know you want to drink deeply from The Successful Coffee House and immediately start putting its principles and Action Day strategies into practice. It is refreshing to read a book that goes far beyond branding and marketing, and covers every aspect of how to enhance your current, or build a new, relevant and profitable retail coffee business in today's market.

This book cuts through the clutter and digs down to the exact core of what specific actions specialty coffee retailers need to take to differentiate their business. I absolutely love the purity and candor of the authors about what does and doesn't work. Best of all, you can finish your first reading of the book in just a few hours.

I give my full and enthusiastic support and encouragement to you, readers of Fresh Cup, and to every other coffee house owner in America to fully digest every word of this book. It is grounded in the best industry practices, and recognizes current and potential future trends that will accelerate your vision to take your brand further and faster, with less effort.

Setting your coffee business apart has evolved into a highly sensory and emotional process. What I enjoy most about this book is its directional clarity in how to create a unique and memorable customer experience, and how to capitalize on all of the senses through holistic branding.

The authors hard earned industry studies and priceless insights will bring you to a whole new level of understanding your competition, and belief in that there has never been a better time to create what they call your "specific brand image."

Jan Weigel
Publisher and President
Fresh Cup Magazine

Authors' Introduction

Absorb the most you can from this book. As you read this book for the first time, choose to commit to a totally open mindset as you turn each page. The right mindset in building your business, like a blueprint for a builder, directs every decision and action as you build.

Would you believe there are people who remember every moment of their lives? Be it a blessing or a curse, the rest of us don't have brains that work like that. However, there is something you can do that will pay huge dividends to your retail coffee business. You can learn and remember from spaced repetition.

We have attempted to incorporate all you will need to inspire and direct the steps to crafting your own Specific Brand Image (SBI). While this book is focused on the coffee house owner, we can't emphasize enough the value for a stand-alone drive-thru, or a café with a drive-thru. Dillanos Customer Joe Lloyd, founder and owner of Durango Joes Coffee in Durango, Colorado, has three traditional walk-in coffee houses, three cafes with drive-thru windows, and three stand alone drive-thrus. Virtually overnight, his business grew daily sales from an average of $1,700 to $2,800 simply by adding a drive-thru window at one of his sit down only cafes.

In your first reading, jot down notes in the margin. Underline and fold back pages with key branding ideas that spark your imagination. If possible, try to read this book cover-to-cover in a single day for your first read-through. Consistent with the learning principles of spaced repetition, during the second reading of this book, one week after your first reading, act on "Today's Action" at the end of each day. Digesting and acting on these keys to building a distinguished and lasting brand, one day at a time, will significantly contribute to the value and direction each action day lends you and your business.

Too many motivational and "how-to" books only provide a momentary distraction before our minds and actions return to business as usual. Most of us, at one time or another, have experienced the great feeling of living with passion for an idea, only to have life's daily routine get in the way a short time later. There is a Tony Robbins quote that comes to mind. "You see, in life, lots of people know what to do, but few people actually do what they know. Knowing is not enough! You must take action." Some of what we are going to tell you to do in this book, you already know. We are fully aware that as you read each of the 22 "action days" you may say to yourself, "I already know about this." We spent more than two decades at many of America's most successful coffee houses, probing for lasting trends and best practices in preparation for crafting this "blueprint for success."

When you consider Dillanos has served as a business development partner to single independent cafes and drive-thrus, as well as large chains since 1992, you can trust we know how to position your business for success. From our national consulting experience, we can tell you that most specialty coffee house owners aren't doing most of what we address in the 22 action days, or there would be more owners full of passion and originality, and more highly distinguished and profitable brands.

The concepts, principles, and keys to success in this book have all been tested, and they work. We have given our all in writing this book, holding nothing back. We share this researched insight when consulting with our customers in order to lead them (and now you) to a unique brand, and industry-leading success. You are guaranteed to find ideas within these pages that will push you from understanding to action. Actually doing what you learn is the proven path to retention, and to creating the results you most desire. When you don't have your own clearly defined goals, and measurable objectives, you don't have your own blueprint. You're allowing just about any trend or idea to sweep you away into somebody else's brand plan. The key to positive change is to continually challenge your thinking.

Commit to becoming one of the best specialty coffee retailers in your community, state, and nation. Embrace all 22 action days as an adventure that will ultimately lead you and your coffee house to exceeding every customer's expectations every day. Now, let's get started on your journey to create your own successful coffee house.

David J. Morris and Chris Heyer

Embracing Holistic Branding

In order to successfully create an exceptional coffee house, you need to first have a thorough understanding of what creates that seemingly elusive perfect customer experience. It all starts with crafting your Specific Brand Image (SBI).

- What is the distinguishing strategy behind the curb appeal of your exterior design?
- What role does coffee aroma play?
- What value do you place on sound?
- How does lighting contribute to the ambience and customer purchases?
- What interior building and design textures create a unique and desired brand personality?
- What role does the sense of touch play in your customer experience?

The overall environment, your staff's emotions, the color accents, and menu concept and content all influence your customer's sensory experience. Branding is everything. Everything is branding. You need to plan how to select each sensory ingredient in order to achieve the optimal synergy for your customers' five senses. In marketing vernacular, this is called holistic branding. This means that you optimize everything the customer sees, tastes, hears, touches, and feels. As we launch into your 22-day action plan, we would like to share our perspective on each of the five senses.

Sight

Sight often overrules the other senses, and has the power to persuade someone to at least explore making an initial purchase from your business based on perceived quality. Let's examine the Starbucks brand visually. While locations are ever changing in exterior and interior design to reflect shifting customer preferences, the company has remained constant in adhering to many of the best practices of holistic branding. While many coffee snobs publicly deny it, even they occasionally seek out a Starbucks on vacation. We all know we can depend on it to offer acceptable, consistently prepared drinks. Through this book, you too can create "corporate confidence" with even a single location coffee house by following the steps in the daily action plans.

Smell

When you walk into a coffee house and smell only waffles, crepes, and strong odors at lunch, you are missing out on the allure of fresh ground coffee's incredible aroma. You can close your eyes, cover your ears, refrain from touch and taste, but still smell when you're in an authentic coffee house.

Smell is the sense we most take for granted, and is incredibly difficult to describe. Just have a cupping with your roaster, and listen as he or she rattles off a list of aromas you can't even begin to sense. To paraphrase Lyall Watson in Jacobson's

Organ, in technical terms, there are receptor cells in the nose. These receptor cells turn chemical information into electrical signals, which travel along the olfactory nerves all the way to the cranial cavity, where they gather in the olfactory bulbs. The olfactory bulbs then feed the cerebral cortex, where association takes place, and nameless signals are transformed into specific aromas. That was the long way around saying it is important to make your coffee house smell like a coffee house, not a restaurant!

Sound

Just as smell is connected to memory, so is sound.. Music mixed with the low buzz of people engaged in casual conversation can't be undervalued. Don't let your baristas select the music of your brand. As an owner, music theme and the mood and energy level it creates is as important as the soundtrack behind your favorite movies. Consider your customer demographics when selecting your morning and evening music. Your music subtly contributes to defining your brand, so make sure to keep your music style consistent from one day to another, and from one location to the next.

Pretend for a moment that your coffee house is a theater stage for a play that begins the second you open the doors. Every cast member knows their part, and works to earn a standing ovation with every performance.

Research has proven that when you listen to music while exercising, you run faster, lift more, and feel better during and after the workout. Music can lift or lower the spirit of your staff and customers. We will be talking more about this a little later, as part of your daily action plans.

Touch

We don't often think about it, but touch is critical to an exceptional customer experience in a coffee house. Doesn't any cappuccino taste better the second your lips touch a perfect porcelain or ceramic cup? This is not to say that paper cups aren't a necessity for your quick-and-go customers, but wouldn't your customers pay more for perfect presentation during an in-store experience? Doesn't Coca-Cola taste better in a glass than in a plastic bottle? Why do you think Starbucks keeps their grocery store Frappuccino bottles glass instead of plastic? The feel of your front counter, solid tables, and comfortable chairs are essential to capitalizing on your customers' sense of touch, and creating the feel of your brand.

Taste

It all starts with your taste buds. It is generally believed that women are more sensitive to taste than men. This is an interesting fact, considering retail specialty coffee attracts up to 20 percent more women than men.

There are four types of taste buds, concentrated in different areas of the tongue. The very tip is best at perceiving sweet taste notes. Sour taste notes are most pronounced on the sides of your tongue. That bitter taste is at the back of your tongue, and saltiness is all over your tongue. All taste is formed from a mixture of these basic elements.

Smell and taste are closely related. We all smell more flavors than we actually taste. When the nose is compromised, perhaps from illness, taste suffers an 80 percent loss. Full sensory appreciation includes appearance (latte art), consistency (perfect steaming and blending of milk with specialty coffee), and temperature.

Now that you have been fully immersed in the opportunities of capitalizing on all your customer's senses, you are ready to begin.

Day 1: Branding is Everything. Everything is Branding.

The biggest hurdle you face in seeing your company's branding opportunities is between your ears. If we could, we would issue you "branding glasses" to see the retail branding world through our eyes. With nothing more important to business success than brand differentiation, we will continually be referencing your own Specific Brand Image (SBI) in almost every one of these brand building action days. We are talking about a totally new beginning, looking at how everything is connected to your brand. It starts with your vision and imagination to see that branding is everything, and everything is branding.

Building a brand isn't easy. It is highly personal. It is literally your life's investment. You have the power to create an incredible customer experience. With the right understanding, you can effectively address everything your customer sees, hears, tastes, touches, and feels. The result? Over-the-top customer loyalty. The best coffee houses in America are equally as committed to premier coffee and preparation quality as they are to letting no customer leave as a nameless stranger.

There are only a handful of retail coffee brands that fully

capitalize on all the senses. We have found that in general, the best holistic branding and personalized service is executed by family-owned businesses with no more than ten locations. We've consulted with many family businesses, as well as small and large retail specialty coffee franchises from coast-to-coast. Too often the owners have a limited understanding or appreciation for experiential retail. Usually it is a husband and wife team who instinctively move way beyond the two-dimensional world of branding (seeing and tasting), into a far more expansive view of what creates a unique customer experience.

As the owner, it all starts and ends with you. You can turn even the smallest details into big branding opportunities. We hear every day, "There's nothing new in my industry that isn't already being done." Had Dwayne Sorenson believed that, there would have never been a Stumptown. Had we believed that, Dillanos Coffee Roasters would have never been born. We turn that misguided and uninspired thinking upside down with many of our customers. Don't ever consider the small things unimportant. You have heard "the brand is in the details." Everything is important in creating your own Specific Brand Image.

We like to start with your café's restroom to help you appreciate how everything is branding, and branding is everything. Is it as sterile and brand-less as you would find in a hospital, or does it capture the texture, color accents, and coffee-centric soul of your brand? You're paying for it. What is stopping you from making every square inch of your space a representation of your brand?

Look at every surface in color and texture, from your ceiling, walls, floors, furniture, wall displays, community boards, and menu, to point of sale, condiment bar, and restroom.

Best Practices Tips

One of our simplest best practices tips is to use your windows exclusively as a branding surface. Take down all taped up promotions, community announcements, and seasonal/signature drinks and food pairing posters that clutter your storefront glass. In some cases, a single posting can be congruent with your SBI. Take advantage by creating clear vinyl clings or stickers of your logo, days and hours open, and possibly a rotating inspiring message or promotion. Keeping the glass clear of clutter is one of the required best practices to give first-time customers confidence in the quality of the experience, products, and service you provide.

It can be difficult to imagine that glass can be a perfect medium for contributing to the emotional power and attraction of your brand. If in doubt, start looking at business storefronts—in every kind of business—to see if they even begin to utilize the branding opportunity they have on their glass. The stock neon "open" sign you purchased at a big box store immediately alerts potential new customers that you are a mom and pop retail coffee business with questionable consistency and quality. The SBI is in the details. Have your "open" sign custom made, i.e. "Durango Joe's is now open."

Whether you have multiple locations, or a single coffee house, it is worth investing in a professional design service to craft your logo and key graphic accompaniments. Most importantly, you and your baristas define the soul of your brand.

Let's hop into the brain of one of the greatest promoters since P.T. Barnum: Evel Knievel. In a former life, I (David) was inspired by Evel Knievel's charisma and daring stunts. I became a BMX bicycle rider. I would compete in national competitions and perform at elementary, junior high, and high school assemblies. Knowing this, you can appreciate why in envisioning the birth of a specialty coffee roaster, my thoughts turned to Evel. If he could, Evel would have bottled and sold the air he breathed. The guy was a natural at understanding that branding is everything, and everything is branding. Evel was bold and original in differentiating himself. What person, or business, sparks your imagination? Think about what inspires you, and about what you can do to be bold and original in differentiating yourself.

TODAY'S ACTION:

Look at the glass on your business storefront, as well as every surface outside and inside your business. Is it treated as the sacred branding surface that defines your space? Is it burdened with anything non-branded? We aren't just talking about your logo. We are talking about everything.

Now, go to your nearest non-coffee national retailer like Jamba Juice, Chipotle, or Panera Bread, and find a seat. Take a deep breath, then slowly soak in everything—the smells in the air, the colors and varied textures on the walls, floor and ceiling, the sounds you hear, and anything branded with a logo, or some identifying graphic.

Begin your second step in awakening to the power of holistic branding in your coffee house by going to a Starbucks, then one or two competing coffee houses. Try to imagine what you would do to better brand everything you see, feel, hear, touch, and smell. After these exercises, you will have a better understanding of what's right and wrong as it applies to holistic branding. Your brand is a powerful selling tool you must first understand, then create, control, and evolve. When you step into the world of holistic branding, over time your brand will take on a meaning to your customers far greater than the sum of its parts.

Day 2: Create a Flexible Brand.

Consider your brand theme the seasoning, and today's most progressive coffee house interior designs the meal. Don't be too thematic in design. Being too thematic in design requires frequent design changes in order to stay relevant. That said, your brand does need to have a distinct personality, with easy update flexibility.

When the Dillanos marketing team works with independent and chain retail coffee house owners, we explain the importance of making the brand yours, while allowing room for change. For example, we have a customer who was determined to make his SBI a Tommy Bahama look, complete with dark wicker, burlap wall coverings below the chair rail, and some artificial palm trees. While we could easily envision his theme idea, we eased him into using his Tommy Bahama atmosphere more subtly, as the seasoning, rather than to be so thematic that there was little room for future change.

Every coffee house owner's SBI should be as unique as their personal passions. This comment usually first elicits a blank, puzzled look on an owner's face. Our other guiding mantra underscores the importance of today's action: Create 80 percent of your design, menu, and customer service based on the industry's best practices. The other 20 percent should be based on your personal passions and ideas from other industries. Nordstrom has a one percent rule. Make your business one percent better than all the competition, and you are on the road to a resonating SBI. We all know Nordstrom lives its mission to make you feel like a VIP with every visit.

The basic approach to brand positioning is not to create something totally new and different, but to manipulate what's already being done by doing it better. The specialty coffee customer is no longer accepting of a predictable, cookie cutter coffee house experience. The result? Many of those businesses are closing, or about to sell to a savvy entrepreneur who sees the potential to create an unforgettable SBI.

The question most frequently asked by existing coffee house owners and many considering entering the retail specialty coffee business is, "Why is there a need for a new approach in branding? There is a Starbucks on just about every corner. With Howard Schultz at the helm, always first in just about everything, how can I trump what the Green Giant is doing?" Starbucks' stated plan is to end all cookie cutter interior designs, and "go local" by having interior thematic design "that captures the soul of communities and neighborhoods" while maintaining their distinctive SBI. Always looking forward, Starbucks is a shining example of creating a flexible brand, while still consistently providing the familiar feeling of security and corporate confidence that you are in a Starbucks.

Before determining your own specialty coffee business model, start an in-depth, Internet study of the best independent and chain coffee houses in America. There is always a list like " The 50 Best Coffee Houses in America." In the process, you will discover that individual twist, or look, that gives "America's best" their SBI. The most common word used today by the best independents to describe their specialty coffee relevance is "craft." The word "handcrafted," used and overused by roasters and coffee retailers of yesteryear has little meaning today. Today, it is all about being dedicated to the craft of roasting and perfect preparation.

When we say "be flexible with your brand," it is all about you, but it needs to be about your customers, too. That Tommy Bahama theme idea was a case where the owner had such a strong personal preference for his idea that he was blinded and confined. The music format he imagined would be the best of the '80s, with Jimmy Buffet and other legends of that music era. Besides the brand and look dating back to the 1980s, the idea just didn't leave any flexibility in tweaking the furniture, interior design, or general feel to remain more relevant to the customer.

While a trend, by definition, lasts up to five years, the specialty coffee industry is on such a fast track of change, you need to update core menu and interior accents about every three years. Roast levels (lighter roasts are the rage at this writing), and manual brewing trends and preferences are changing constantly. We'd like to get your creative juices flowing by highlighting the design evolution of Woods Coffee in Bellingham, Washington. When Dillanos started roasting for Woods Coffee Founder Wes Herman, he had a 650-square-foot coffee house that shared a wall and parking lot with a service station, plus a small drive-thru. Fast forward to 2015, and Woods Coffee has won the "Best in Western Washington" award three years in a row. Today, Wes and his family have grown to twelve incredibly profitable and preferred coffee houses in the northern Washington region. Local customer preference for Woods Coffee has led to strip mall owners, grocery chains, and commercial real estate owners asking for a new Woods Coffee House instead of a Starbucks in a three-city radius. Having a great affinity for nature and a natural talent for envisioning a unique and flexible brand, Wes styled his first three coffee houses after a warm and inviting Alpine ski lodge. The sea green and light chocolate wall colors were complemented by a light knotty pine chair rail and lower wall paneling. He found a local metal artisan to create Woods' unique rustic metal lighting fixtures. He also found and negotiated a reasonable price for a breathtaking natural wood table and window counters with "live" edges (naturally jagged), long before they were mainstream in other independent coffee houses. With each new coffee house Woods has opened in the last four years, customers see an evolution of the brand textures, colors, menu, and furniture without ever losing the original concept. Being tuned into industry trends, Wes has gone back to his original coffee houses to make subtle changes.

Fortune 500 companies have long understood they need to make contemporary brand changes and enhancements at least every five years. Now, successful smaller business and entrepreneurs are matching that pace.

TODAY'S ACTION:

Fresh Cup Magazine now has a section every month dedicated to the latest coffee house interior and menu design trends. If you haven't done so already, order a subscription to Fresh Cup, Tea and Coffee Trade Journal, and Barista magazine. If you already subscribe to these magazines, read the most recent issues cover to cover today, and commit to doing the same with every issue. They serve as your cutting-edge research department to ensure you stay in step with the ever-evolving specialty coffee scene. Your baristas would really benefit from reading these industry magazines as well, in order to get a sense of the importance of their role in the coffee community, and to inspire them to view their role as more than a job, but a passion.

Day 3: Be Unique, but Not Odd.

We too often see retail coffee businesses, particularly single location cafes and drive-thrus, where the owner thinks a fun play on words for their name sets them apart. One of our favorites is "Java the Hut." Obviously, the owner is referring to Jabba the Hutt, a memorable character in Star Wars. Another example of being odd is a two-location coffee house on the west coast that went from an It's a Grind franchise to an independent owner. With every good intention of getting attention, he named his coffee houses, "Espresso 4 U." Needless to say, they aren't in business any more. However, don't mistake steering clear of "being odd" for meaning you want a pedestrian name and look to your business. Who would have thought Blue Bottle or Mad Cap Coffee would be acceptable names? Who would have thought it would be a good idea to call a technology company Apple?

The key to being unique, and not just odd, is being uncompromising in your commitment to quality. Portland born and based Stumptown Coffee has proven this with an uncompromising stand on sourcing superior and unique coffees. They require perfect preparation, which instantly created word of mouth that resulted in long lines of customers. These hordes of fans were willing to pay more than they've ever paid before for a coffee drink.

Draw a line in the sand. Great coffee houses have a point of view, not just beverage and food businesses. You have to believe in something. A strong stand is how you attract super fans. These fans defer to you for coffee knowledge, and even defend your business, because your brand has become part of their personal identity. They spread the word further and more passionately than any traditional marketing could ever accomplish.

How proud are your customers to defend what you've created? Keep in mind that strong points of view can turn some people off. As with Stumptown in the early years, the baristas were justifiably accused of being arrogant, aloof, and even dismissive of their customers. While Stumptown's retail environment has eased into being a bit friendlier, it still boldly stands for uncompromising quality. When you and your baristas don't know what you believe and where you draw the line, everything becomes a compromise. Be willing to lose a handful of customers if it means that the majority of your customers love you and your menu offerings intensely.

In the grocery category, there has been a huge identity crisis that has caused many chains to send mixed messages to customers as to whether they represent quality, or price reductions. Chains like Whole Foods and Sprouts Fresh Markets are growing like crazy. We all know that Whole Foods isn't the most competitively priced, but it stands for selling the highest quality natural and organic products available. Whole Foods' vision and mission is clear. This means the food may often be more expensive, but it is one of the most profitable grocery chains in America, with a pronounced and loyal following.

There is a world of difference between truly standing for something and saying you stand for something, but having staff and customers who don't believe it. Standing for something isn't just about writing it down in a business plan or employee manual. It's about believing it, and living it with every customer experience.

TODAY'S ACTION:

If you are in a densely populated city, spend no less than 30 minutes in specialty coffee competitor locations, including Starbucks. Jot down their strengths and weaknesses. If your business is in a small town, visit all community competitors. Seek out what is different, odd, and/or unique to each coffee house and drive-thru. Try to define their SBI. For example, Starbucks' stated SBI is to provide consistency in all they serve, and to be the community gathering place.

Day 4: Learn From Other Industries.

Harley – Davidson does not sell motorcycles. Starbucks does not sell coffee. They sell an experience. If you haven't yet, read Howard Schultz's book, Pour Your Heart Into It: How Starbucks Built a Company One Cup at a Time. Looking at many industries as he built Starbucks, Howard decided he wanted to create "a Starbucks way of life." Schultz articulated his vision into what he called "the third place." There is home, work, and Starbucks. Whether it is a few minutes at the airport, an hour-and-a-half reading the Sunday newspaper, or writing a book, Starbucks is where he imagined you would be, at home and on the road.

Birth of "Craft" Coffee

The moment online communication and social media exploded, it rearranged our relationship landscape. Now, rather than seeking out just a meeting space, we're using cafés as our "second office." It's our place to plug in to our online community, catch up on work, and most importantly, enjoy the newly appreciated craftsmanship of fine specialty coffees. Craft breweries, small batch distilleries, and boutique wine bars opened the doors for coffee and tea to carve out their own artisan category of dedicated followers who appreciate the subtle nuances of rare and exquisite coffees and blends.

Most of us are familiar with the usual suspects on the trendy coffee scene and should totally immerse ourselves in what they are doing best: preparing the finest craft beverages, and building customer traffic.

The last thing the market needs is a late coming "me too" operation. Consumers are seeking out new, original, and highly personalized experiences. Harley-Davidson is an experience that helps define your spirit. This change in Harley's persona turned it from a dying company into a thriving lifestyle brand for all demographics.

New ideas in developing your own SBI can be fueled by retailers like Restoration Hardware and Apple. These brands have had a recognizable influence on the authentic character in coffeehouse interior design the past few years. Explore the story and experience of other brands to infuse fresh ideas into your coffee business. It is fascinating to awaken to the power of color in branding. Coca-Cola owns red, Tiffany & Co. owns robin egg blue, Starbucks owns green, and UPS with its "What can brown do for you?" campaign has cemented its ownership of brown. The same kind of color ownership applies to Home Depot with orange and Apple with white. As you visit other retailers in your daily life, start viewing everything through a new lens. What is the experience like? There is so much more than customer service to notice.

Coffee houses attract more women than men. Women are naturally more attuned to an experience. They don't buy brands. They join them. The same can be said of the millennial generation. They want to belong to a group, or culture, which allows them to commit to a cause with authentic passion and drive.

We have saved the wine industry as our last and most relevant industry exploration recommendation. How often have you heard that coffee is just like wine? These words usually stem from understandable industry comparisons. Much like coffee, the flavor of wine is affected by soil, altitude and other climate factors. Coffee and wine are both made from agricultural products. The fruits are comparably small, sweet, round, and best harvested ripe. There is a season for harvesting and processing for both. Both can be identified by variety and origin, and both industries use many of the same terms to describe sensory perception.

Baristas can learn a lot from the best wine sommeliers who are able to passionately describe the flavor notes and any specifics that lend appreciation for a wine's origin

TODAY'S ACTION:

Focus on leading wine brands via their websites. While researching, seek out parallels and original ideas you could incorporate in enhancing, or creating your SBI. Note how winemakers romance origin, taste, and what differentiates that company's wine from competitors.

Once you have this eye-opening awareness through your research, begin making it a practice to see the retail brands around you as more than just their logo. Think about what differentiates each brand from the next.

Day 5: Differentiate Your Brand

One of the common questions we hear from customers across the country is, "How can I make my coffee house stand out from the competition?" With so many roasters and retailers committed to uncompromising quality, it can seem tough to get out of the "me too" mindset. When we look back to Starbucks and other coffee chains, the primary goal was to focus on centralized standardization. This template provided the security of a consistent customer experience. There was also a significant cost savings from centralized purchasing. Today, however, no customer appreciates a one size fits all model. Every coffee house you build should have local and brand distinguishing differences.

Differentiation is one of the most important strategic and tactical activities in which you must constantly engage. What are the demographics of your primary customer base at each location? What opportunities do those demographics provide?

The following examples of brand differentiation are provided to inspire you to create your own unique ways of setting your brand apart from the competition.

Differentiate by Neighborhood

Recognizing the powerful trend of everything local, Starbucks has focused its café design mission on incorporating the city and neighborhood feel into each new location. The mission is to make "local differences" in every new Starbucks in the world. No more cookie cutter floor plans. Once again, Schultz is following the independent coffee house's lead. Now, authenticity not only comes from your depth of understanding of the coffee process from seed to cup, but also your ability to give your coffee house a touch of local charm.

Differentiate by Doing Good

Being a socially conscious brand is no longer optional. You are, or will be bombarded with schools, churches, and a plethora of other worthy causes looking for your support. Consider what you personally care about most, then what your customers care about, and finally what you can do to connect with and support an industry cause.

Don't get lost in the mindset of offering free coffee to every organization that asks. It is not sustainable, and it waters down your cause-based image to the point where you won't be taken seriously. The point is to pick one, or two causes that reflect the core of your beliefs and your business. Allocate all your humanitarian efforts and resources to this single or dual focus. The more single-minded you become with your philanthropic affiliation, the more seriously your customers will take your efforts, and the more your voice will be recognized in the community as a company who gives back to a cause greater than themselves.

Differentiate by Time of Day

Anthem Coffee and Tea in Puyallup, Washington decided to build an evening business by branding it "Anthem after 5," with a large clear window cling announcement on the glass beside the front door. Every evening at 5 o'clock, the coffee house becomes a live music, movie, or special event venue with a short appetizer menu and an intentionally limited selection of Washington wines and local microbrews. Anthem's owner, Bryan Reynolds, has seen a remarkable increase in his evening business as a result.

Differentiate by Customer Segment

Harley-Davidson expanded its customer base while remaining true to its SBI by appealing to potential niche buyers, like women, through design, creative marketing, and social media. According to the most recent statistics by SCAA, 58 percent of specialty coffee house customers are women. Michael Maller, owner of Espresso Cielo in Palm Springs, California, capitalizes on these demographics by adding a high tea every Sunday during the busiest tourist months of the year. Since first offering this unique coffeehouse experience, every seat has been filled. The high tea is offered at a fixed price, and a limited selection of teas and appropriate English tea sandwiches and sweets are served.

Differentiate by Focusing on the Experience

Starbucks originally focused on the "romance and theater" of coffee houses. This was essential to Starbucks' creation and rapid rise to success. While Starbucks has mostly automated the espresso preparation process, Howard Schultz has brought them back to the party overnight, making customer service far more personalized by requiring baristas to state the customer's name twice: once when an order is placed, to write the name on the cup, and once calling out the name when the drink is ready. The huge side benefit to this customer service strategy is that it better ensures drink order accuracy.

We have only scratched the surface of ways you can build a unique SBI by being different than the competition.

TODAY'S ACTION:

Make your own list of what you can do to differentiate your brand. Don't be afraid to adopt the best practices of your competition while exploring unique differentiation ideas. Armed with fresh eyes from your study of your competitors and other retail businesses, you will begin to get fresh ideas that will contribute to forming your SBI.

Day 6: Make all Decisions with Your Customer in Mind.

We just warned against being "me too" with your SBI. However, you must also be careful not to be too forward thinking for your customer base. All too often we run into business owners who are so excited to join the coffee-centric third, or even fourth wave, that they miss out entirely on the core customer base in the community they're trying to influence. Bring artfully crafted coffees to the masses, and share your passion for the culinary coffee experience, while beginning to educate your customers.

Serving single cup pour over during the morning rush may not be appreciated by your customers who rely on quick service for their morning cup of brewed coffee. Conversely, progressive communities in downtown Seattle or Los Angeles aren't going to be very impressed with the coffee house that lacks deeply trained baristas serving seasonal single origin coffees via an alternative brew method.

Your passion for great coffee at any price may not immediately align with the interest of your target customer. We learned this difficult lesson when we went to the Caribbean several years ago to visit a customer of ours, Rituals Coffee. Rituals is a chain of seventy coffee houses within the islands of Trinidad, Saint Lucia, and Saint Kitts. When we first arrived, our goal was to meet with all of the baristas as part of a nine day, eight hour per day training session. The purpose was to bring the U.S. coffee business model and customer service concept to the Caribbean culture.

We were confident we could turn their coffee business around in nine days of extensive training because it was a tried-and-true method we had used dozens of times with coffee house chains in the states. What we neglected to recognize was the drastic cultural differences that bled through to the shy and passive way the Rituals staff related to each other and their customers. We also underestimated the cultural preference for tea over coffee. Most importantly, we also had to consider the Caribbean's high temperatures and humidity. The number one selling beverages were cold non-coffee smoothies, called "chillers." Our training wasn't as successful as it could have been because we weren't aware of regional preferences.

Since our first Rituals training, we've been able to slowly introduce cold brew coffee to their customers, nearly doubling coffee sales in just three years. With "real" coffeehouse chains entering Trinidad today, Rituals is beginning to see a spike in hot and cold brewed coffee sales. Rituals customers are still at least a year away from appreciating the taste and price of single origin coffees. We learned we had to move only as fast as the culture itself would allow. No amount of our own passion for coffee could have changed that dynamic.

When sifting through the details of your marketing plan analysis, consider your core audience, your competition, and recognize what is underrepresented in your current market. There is a fine line between trying to fill gaps with your unique SBI, and overwhelming your community base by doing things that don't relate to your potential customers. Explore the receptivity of your customer base before you begin to embrace the latest trends in specialty coffee.

If you want to be the first to introduce a unique craft-centric coffee concept to a community, that's great, but do so with your customer in mind. Palace Coffee Company recently opened a specialty coffee shop in Amarillo, Texas. Amarillo is probably one of the least likely places to accept the concept of a slow brew bar, or single origin espresso drinks. The owner, Patrick Burns, having grown up in West Texas, knew his audience would struggle with the forward thinking coffee style. Rather than forcing his audience to taste coffee the way he wanted them to, he embraced the fact that they may be wary of the trendy approach to coffee preparations, alternative brew methods, and higher pricing.

His mission in the first month of business was to personally welcome each customer as they walked in the shop and overwhelm them with West Texas hospitality. Burns then walked them through their coffee choices comfortably. He immediately took the worry, or fear out of the craft coffee initiation process with every customer.

By being customer-centric, he is quickly developing a loyal, coffee-focused following in an area previously not exposed to specialty coffee education and offerings. Based on long-standing customer preferences, he still sells the sweet, syrupy drinks to the customers who ask for them. This savvy business owner knows it will take patience and time to get some of his customer base excited about the latest craft coffee drink offerings.

TODAY'S ACTION:

Do an online search as well as an on site analysis of all the coffee shops in your competitive radius. Evaluate if your SBI is unique enough to stand on its own, or if it is so unique that it won't be accepted by your target customers.

Create an action plan of ways to graduate your core clientele to a place where they will embrace your SBI differentiation. Your passion can, and should be embraced as part of what makes your SBI unique. Be careful to ease your customers into your world in a comfortable way, without trying to redefine their coffeehouse experience too quickly.

Day 7: Hire the Right Employees

What a simple statement, right? It seems obvious enough, but you'd surprised at how often many of us are guilty of making poor hiring choices. These choices ultimately impact the business, our customers, our staff, and our bottom line.

How do we avoid these mistakes? Hire great employees, not just good employees. In Jim Collins' international bestseller, Good to Great, he discusses the fact that good is the enemy of great. This is no less true when seeking out a barista to fill a role on your team. To be fair, this industry seems to have an overly high annual turnover rate of 70 percent. Usually the person stuck covering the shifts of a fired, or chronically absent employee, is you. No one has the time to handle the unexpected six-hour shift.

In hiring, don't look for the fastest and easiest way out. It will cost you much more in the long run to hire the wrong employee. The wrong employee hurts your current staff members because they're stuck with a co-worker who could bring down the morale and culture of the entire team and even your customer base. The amount of training, time, and resources you invest in that employee hurts your bottom line more than anything else. Consider the following.

- Have you checked their references? It is so important to check with both former employers and personal references. Often times, baristas will be fired for theft from one shop, only to be hired by their closest competition days later. Make the phone calls and ask your baristas what they have heard, if the applicant is a former barista. When talking to former employers, make sure you ask the question, "Would you rehire this person?"
- Google their name and check out their Facebook, Twitter, Instagram, and any other social media accounts. This may seem over-the-top, but it can provide valuable clues as to their character and values.
- Is the employee innately positive and excited to talk to people without prompting, or is he or she simply a fast barista with the skill set you need? It's easy to train a personable employee into an amazing barista, but you can never turn a wonderful latte artist with a negative attitude into an amazing employee.
- One way to check for true personality before you hire is to bring a few of the potential baristas in as a group to interview before you open at six in the morning. The first test is if they are on time and engaging. Allow them to sit in a section of the café for at least fifteen minutes while you subtly evaluate their interactions with one another before beginning the interview process. Some of them will keep their heads down, scanning for email or text messages to avoid eye contact. Others will fold their arms, looking anywhere but at the person next to them. Hopefully, one or two in the group will default to naturally sunny and talkative personalities. These are the superstars you want to hire.
- Ask the right questions! Dive in to understanding what motivates your barista, how they like working with oth-

ers, what makes them frustrated, and what hours they're available. Don't wait until they're hired to find out that they have classes from 9:00 to 11:00 a.m. every weekday or that they get stressed in high-volume environments. Create a list of core questions that bring out these potential issues from the beginning.

• Once you find the perfect employee, ensure they're getting great training from the start. If all you're looking for is previous experience, you're relying on what someone else may or may not have done in terms of training.

On their first day, spend no less than an hour going over their job description, your expectations, and any non-negotiable rules. Each employee must understand from the beginning what defines success for you and your business.

TODAY'S ACTION:

If you haven't done so already, create a 3-4 page employee handbook that outlines the basic structure of policies and procedures for your company. Make sure you go over this handbook with every one of your current employees. You can find basic outlines online, or contact Dillanos and ask for a template. You will want to customize your employee handbook to clearly communicate your vision. This is the first step in making every customer experience so exceptional and inviting that they cannot wait to return.

Your next step today is to evaluate your current staff and shift manager, without prejudice, or favoring tenure, or preparation expertise. Do you have even one staff member who is bringing your culture down? Do you have leaders in place who bring down your entire team? Take feedback seriously. If a customer is willing to complain about an employee, the situation is likely more serious than you realize. Make the difficult decision to fire these poor performers now.

Day 8: You Had Me at Hello

The problem with most coffee houses today is the owner's transactional mentality. Successful specialty coffee houses embrace experiential retail. Bryan Reynolds from Anthem Coffee & Tea in Puyallup, Washington announces your presence the moment you walk through the door. From opening day, he made sure every customer was personally greeted. Newcomers and regulars were so immediately welcomed that Anthem quickly became the community's second home. While Bryan is committed to extensive barista training and high quality standards, his endearing customer engagement is the driving reason Anthem has been so successful. Bryan is realizing industry high profits, despite initial naysayers and the failed business history of his distressed and aging small community downtown business district. Anthem added over 700 square feet to his originally 1500 square-foot coffeehouse to keep up with the demand. Bryan keeps his team engaged all day long with over-the-top fun, yet requires high personal accountability.

Being playful with your staff and customers is one of the most motivating ways to create a loyal following. The old "Cheers" mentality of wanting to belong to an environment where "everybody knows your name" is a timeless sentiment that will always ring true. Make it a priority to create that same environment in your coffee house.

The first step is to start paying more attention to what Dale Carnegie calls "the sweetest and most important sound in any language:" the customer's name. The moment the customer hears his or her name, it makes them feel like your place is their place. It invites them to forget the daily grind. They can just focus on the excitement of living in in the moment. They are someone who matters, not just a drink buyer on an assembly line of coffee transactions.

It is easy to create your own "Cheers" environment with the following steps:

- Every customer is greeted within the first five seconds of walking in the door.
- Everyone is welcomed as they reach the counter
- Your barista uses the customer's name at least three times
- Every customer is thanked with a genuine parting phrase. "Good to see you, Dave!" is much more personal and authentic than, "Have a nice day."
- Model and create a caring culture. Do this correctly, and you will no longer have customers, you will have friends who come to be part of a community.

This may seem lofty and idealistic, but it's completely attainable when you work from a strategic game plan. Start by encouraging your staff to learn the names of your regular customers. Buy a notebook for every staff member. Have each barista keep track of his or her own notebook. As they meet new customers, they introduce themselves first, and then ask for the customer's name so they can write the name on the drink being crafted for them. The barista then quickly writes down the name of that customer, something memorable about them, and their drink in their own notebook as a way to track all their customers. If you are able to see the customer's car as they park, or pull up, write down their car model. When you see this car pull into the lot, you can begin making their drink before they've even walked in the door! This "name game" should be listed as a requirement in your barista's job description. Imagine how at home your customers will feel when every barista has memorized not just their drink type, but their name as well.

TODAY'S ACTION:

Buy enough Moleskines, or similar notebooks, for each of your staff members. Start having baristas record the names and drinks of all their customers. After several weeks, hold a staff meeting. Tell your baristas they have one minute to write down the names and associated drinks of as many customers as they can remember. Give them $1 for every name and drink combination they write down. This creates a fun competition for your staff, and even better, it creates a memorable environment for your customers.

Day 9: Staff and Self-Education

Gone are the days of "barista" meaning an entry level, minimum wage position. Being a committed and well-trained barista today can be a profitable career. There is a growing demand for coffee-centric baristas, and career opportunities are building momentum every day. As the specialty coffee market rapidly matures, the most successful coffee house owners invest in their best baristas. The importance of barista education is rapidly building.

There is always another aspect of the industry to learn.
As the owner, you should have a close relationship with your roaster. They should lead you in understanding the meticulous process of importing, grading, quality control, and cupping. Ask your roaster if you can join them, at your expense, on a trip to origin. Your experience is worth so much more to your staff and customers than the cost of your trip.

No coffee house owner today can afford to remain stagnant while the industry continues to evolve. Every minute and dollar invested in coffee education for both you and your baristas can return many times your investment.

Throughout the '90s and early 2000s, the barista's preparation responsibilities were mostly limited to serving drip coffee, and preparing espresso based beverages. More recently, some cafes have eliminated drip coffee altogether and are exclusively offering single cup methods such as espresso, pour over, Aeropress, Chemex, and other handcrafted options.

The shift from full batch to single cup brewing has been one of the most brand distinguishing strategies that trendy retailers have used to maximize their customer's taste experience while raising prices. Today, every coffee house owner and head barista trainer will benefit from being extremely knowledgeable in more than one alternative brewing method.

Speed in service must be incorporated into implementing any industry trend. Initiating a single-brew program may not be the right choice for every retailer without a few minor tweaks to the customer line flow. Why not set up a separate "slow bar" for the customer willing to wait for the perfect cup of coffee? The correct placement of your "slow bar" will allow time for your barista to interact more with the customer as well. Even in the busiest cafes, counter space can be found for a minimal single cup brew bar. It can be as simple as setting up space at the end of the counter. It needs to be fully understood that changing from batch brew to alternative brew should be an evolution, not revolution. It can slow down service, requiring an adjustment process for everyone involved, including your customers.

While it is important that your training continually evolves, don't think of introducing new trends as an all or nothing decision. Given the right back-of-counter ergonomics, and the ability to face the customers as your barista prepares each cup, you might choose to provide this option only during certain times of the day. Many cafés select quieter times, frequently after the morning and lunch rush. The added benefit is that it is also a great brand enhancing way to increase your retail sales of whole bean coffee.

Besides insisting on latte art, consider the importance of

presentation. Your customers will instantly value the attention to detail when their drink is served in a porcelain cup, placed on a saucer, and accompanied by a demitasse spoon and small glass of sparkling water to cleanse the palate.

The best baristas today are seeking out coffee house owners who will ensure in-depth education, along with opportunities for advancement. Gregory's Coffee is a perfect example. Bailey Arnold, Director of Coffee Education for the progressive Manhattan chain, is in charge of hiring for all of Gregory's highly profitable coffee houses. She reads at least a dozen resumes every week. She notes general negativity or passivity about learning when they write, watching for phrases like "I already know." This is the first red flag that the job candidate will be difficult to teach and have too little appreciation for the depth of knowledge required.

Unfortunately, most coffee house owners today are still operating on the limited knowledge required to profitably grow in the '90s. They are genuinely puzzled as to why their bottom line keeps sinking every year. They blame the lack of profitability on everything from the economy and cost of goods to a poor location. They fail to realize they need to always keep pace with the quickly evolving industry.

It all starts with your passion for and pursuit of continual coffee education through both your roaster and other industry resources. Your dedication to learning and growing will be instrumental in attracting the best baristas in your community.

The nation is waking up to the fact that being a barista can now be a respectable and well compensated profession. Make it your mission to ensure you and your baristas commit to ongoing industry education. Examples of opportunities include:

- Networking with baristas from neighboring coffee houses at local throw downs.
- Attending national, or regional coffee industry confer-

ences (www.coffeefest.com and www.scaa.org).
- Committing the time to make the most of any barista training provided by your roaster.
- Buying a subscription to Barista Magazine for each of your baristas, and making it required reading. As an owner, besides reading Barista Magazine yourself, subscribe and read every issue of Fresh Cup Magazine.
- Having all of your baristas go online and become active participants at www.baristaexchange.com, and regularly visiting www.sprudge.com to learn about the latest industry news.

A fitting example of a clear focus on training and education is Dillanos customer Laila Ghambari, Director of Coffee for Cherry Street Coffee in Seattle. She was crowned the 2014 United States Barista Champion. Laila is credited with developing effective training programs for Seattle's Café Ladro and Cherry Street's growing number of coffee houses. She divided her barista educational training into the following steps:

- Assessing the level of each barista's customer relations and coffee preparation skills.
- Creating coffee education and preparation standards.
- Integrating a system of monitoring barista performance.

As Barista Magazine Editor, Sarah Allen, pointed out in one of her engaging magazine editorials, "In the specialty coffee industry, we talk about the need for owner and barista education all of the time. Tragically, few owners understand its critical importance to success and growth."

TODAY'S ACTION:

Contact your roaster to explore educational coffee training

opportunities for yourself and lead baristas. Go online and explore roasters to determine the depth of their business development support.

After reading and acting on Day 11, you will be ready to better define your, and your baristas', initial and ongoing educational needs. Your mission is to never stop growing in your coffee education. Keep pace with the latest trends in specialty coffee.

Day 10: Educate Your Customers

Always stay connected to your customers' desires and expectations. Have your baristas start introducing your customers to quality coffees and education by discussing what they care about most: roast level and flavor notes. For single origin coffees, if asked, every barista should be able to offer a couple of distinctive points about the coffee's origin.

Consider highlighting a different coffee every week. We have found Friday from 2 p.m. to 3 p.m. is a perfect time slot. Try a variety of brewing methods, including French press, AeroPress, or pour-over to help accentuate certain characteristics with each coffee selection.

Every single detail that makes up the customer experience needs to be rooted in hospitality. Your goal is that every person who walks through your door immediately feels welcome and comfortable. This should be evident long before your barista takes their order, or makes any attempt to educate them about coffee. Your key mission is that nobody leaves a stranger.

Your morning shift manager should take on the role of hospitality leader and coffee trainer. To simplify the lead trainer role, work with your roaster to create a train-the-trainer program. This allows for ongoing, updated, and industry certified training programs.

Your next step is that every customer knows that the owner and each staff member has extensive knowledge, and a love of the industry and the coffees they serve. The journey into coffee education needs to be personalized to your customer's level of interest. As they settle in on their favorite coffee offerings, they will naturally begin to seek out more information about the coffees they enjoy. Tell the story of the coffee, and answer their questions, but get too specific with your customers, and you can quickly lose their interest.

Proactive customer education can add strong coffee appreciation to your core customer base. Have weekly open tastings for customers with your baristas. These events slowly bring out customer questions and taste preferences. Whether in a cupping at your roaster or a tasting at your coffee house, typical flavor descriptors for coffees can be as bewildering as they are helpful. With taste palettes and origin flavor understandings all over the board, some coffee-centric baristas struggle to detect taste characteristics. Just a handful of seasoned tasters can easily differentiate even subtle flavor notes. Have your roaster offer "sound bite" descriptions of the dominant flavor notes, origin, and any story that goes along with the coffee you serve. Require your baristas to memorize these quick descriptions.

Randomly ask every barista to describe the flavor of your blends and single origins. At the weekly customer tastings, taste and re-taste your coffee lineup several times and at different temperatures.

Nothing is more powerful than these scheduled weekly customer coffee tastings. Often, events like these are inappropriately called "cuppings." A true cupping is where professional tasters go around a table and slurp from spoons to determine and rate acidity, body, flavor, and aftertaste, as well as identify inconsistencies from cup to cup. Cuppings are conducted using a specific brewing process. This is generally an advanced exercise and not appropriate for the average consumer.

Whole Bean Coffee Sales

Weekly coffee tastings and featured coffees also serve as sound strategies to sell whole bean coffees featured that week. Baristas should be coached to articulate the story behind the coffee being tasted. Customers will appreciate learning about flavor notes that distinguish the coffee. Place a few bags of the coffee at the customer tasting table to contribute to selling your higher priced single origin coffees.

Selling more whole bean coffee should be an objective of every coffee house owner. While there are exceptions, whole bean sales generally account for less than five percent of total sales. Buying a bag of whole bean coffee is always an event, especially for beginning specialty coffee drinkers. Instead of leaving your coffee beginners to choose between "oaky, apricot, and clove" and "white grape, kiwi, and cantaloupe," know that most customers better relate to simpler descriptors like "chocolaty and nutty" and "citrus, with honey notes." Your baristas need to know the flavors that will easily resonate with your customers. These descriptors serve as a helpful guide to new and experienced specialty coffee drinkers.

The weekly tastings are an opportunity for your baristas as well as for your customers, so regardless of whether there are two, twelve, or even zero customers attending, have your baristas take turns leading the tasting. This gives them a learning opportunity, as they practice articulating the stories and flavor notes of every coffee your café serves. To ensure the integrity and continuity of these weekly tastings, begin by attending and leading the tastings for the first four weeks. Thereafter, attend the tastings at least once a month to ensure they do not become simply chores to be checked off, but remain valuable, fun, and engaging. Regularly scheduled weekly tastings are a disciplined opportunity to share passion and information about the coffees your baristas serve every day.

The last key element in customer education is point of sale support for all of the coffees served. Recognize that displaying origin, roast, and a brief relatable flavor description is key in customer coffee education. You will note that Starbucks strategically places chalkboard signs in wicker coffee bins and on the countertop by single origin whole bean coffees offered that month. Origin, roast, and flavor are all you will see on Starbucks whole bean offerings. Your best customer coffee educator and selling vehicle is an engaging barista, but your signage and menu come in a close second.

TODAY'S ACTION:

Commit and schedule open tastings once a week. If you don't already have simple, repeatable sound bites created for each of your coffees, then call your roaster and arrange a tasting. Consider having your shift managers and baristas join you. Tell your roaster you would like to be provided with customer friendly flavor profiles of each coffee you serve. To ensure that you have an in depth understanding of all the coffees you serve, have your roaster's Director of Coffee describe the growing region or farm, as well as every step in growing and crafting each coffee tasted.

Day 11: Keep Expanding Your Barista's Role

Owners need to invest more than ever before to realize maximum bottom line profits, while building a sustainable business. In this action day, we will discuss the perfect barista resume.

Today's most relevant baristas should have an in-depth knowledge of all menu offerings. Have all of your baristas taste every food and beverage item you serve. As fundamental as this sounds, it is seldom done. Baristas should be authentically suggesting their personal favorite drink and food pairing favorites for each time of day. This one requirement will help increase the amount of your average transaction.

Be engaged in the local and national barista community. Encourage participation in local latte art throwdowns if they are held in your area. Your baristas will hone their latte art skills in a friendly, yet competitive and pride-building atmosphere. Consider hosting your own throwdown. It's a great way to reach out to the barista community and show your staff that you're eager to support and ignite their passion for coffee.

All your baristas need instructions on how to pour perfect

latte art with every cup served, even in to-go cups. Latte art is now a staple of a craft driven coffee house. Incentivize and reward those baristas who excel in perfecting latte art. There are great YouTube instructional videos available to help your baristas as they practice. Ask your roaster to assist in hands-on training with your staff to give them the basics. Be patient, but insistent, as it will take time to perfect pouring latte art.

Introduce single cup brewing methods. Settle on one or two that all your baristas need to master. Start with the perfect pour over. These single-cup demonstrations serve as a way to sell higher margin drinks, especially to your traditional drip coffee drinker. They are also an effective strategy to sell more retail bags of the coffee being offered.

TODAY'S ACTION:

Outline a progressive barista certification program. Each level can include certain sets of achievements including mastering the basics, latte art, and manual brew options. With each level of completion, reward your baristas with a cash bonus, or a symbol of accomplishment. Starbucks created the black apron for the highest level of barista accomplishment. Keep your baristas excited to move to the next level through your appreciation and recognition among their peers.

Day 12: The Evolution of Barista Basics Training

Today's most recognized specialty coffee retailers are gaining national press by being "craft" focused. While the term "craft" is taking on many meanings, it is grounded in a commitment to premium quality coffee sourcing and beverage preparation. Perfect preparation and this commitment to "craft" are supported by in depth barista education.

In the past, an understanding of the story behind each cup was rarely even on the owner's radar screen, much less the barista's. The barista's coffee knowledge was generally limited to knowing the name of the roaster, and being aware of the roast level of coffee they served. Training was usually completed in a few hours, or a few days. Engagement in a greater barista community was seldom seen.

The best wholesale specialty coffee roasters have direct farm relationships to ensure quality and consistency at a fair price. Your roaster should be able to fully immerse your baristas in the seed-to-cup journey.

Today, an extreme example of barista training is exemplified at Seattle's Vivace, founded by internationally recognized David

Schomer. Schomer has a six-month barista apprenticeship requirement. While his commitment to barista education and preparation is considered extreme, the following glimpse into the depth of his café's program will illustrate the possibilities in terms of barista training.

- Schomer begins with required reading to help baristas gain a total understanding of the history of coffee.
- Every barista must know and have a genuine appreciation for the seed-to-cup journey.
- New baristas join in extensive tastings to understand the flavor notes of every coffee Vivace serves. This is all before the barista is introduced to coffee equipment, and the science of extraction.
- Schomer's interpretation of customer service is listening closely to what his customers order, then exceeding expectations in preparation and presentation. At Vivace, the time required for exemplary preparation is accepted as necessary to create perfection in every cup.

Milstead & Co. Coffee is widely considered a "must-experience" coffee house in Seattle. Andrew Milstead is a former U. S. Barista Champion. At the time of this writing, Milstead has been open less than three years, and is already recognized as one of the best coffee houses in America. Andrew's barista apprenticeship lasts three months before a new staff member is free to serve customers without supervision.

Both Vivace and Milstead are busy from the moment they open their doors until they close. There are no apologies for higher prices based on a commitment to the perfectly prepared cup and presentation.

While these long-term training examples may seem extreme, they serve to highlight the dramatic evolution of barista "basics." A more common approach to training is to select a lead trainer for each of your coffee houses. Every new hire should spend at least twenty hours on coffee education, equipment instruction, and preparation training before being allowed to serve customers.

Many Dillanos customers across the country initially fear their nearby Starbucks. The main question they ask is, "How can I compete with the green giant?" Our number one answer is, "Utilize the resources available to you." Have your roaster provide in depth teaching for you and your lead trainer. Both of you should learn all about the seed-to-cup process to fully appreciate the art and science that goes into every bean.

The majority of your customers will have first tasted espresso-based beverages at Starbucks where all espresso drinks are made on super-automatic machines for speed and consistency. At your coffee house, these beverages will be hand crafted. In addition to dramatically enhancing the taste from top to bottom with perfectly textured milk, every drink should be capped with the beauty of a poured rosetta. Craft retailers have every barista master single cup brewing methods to bring out the best flavors from exceptional single origin coffees. These simple measures immediately separate your business from Starbucks and your "old school" coffee house competition.

To ensure Dillanos' focus on customer success, all of our resources and energies are customer driven. In recent years, we have created a department dedicated exclusively to consulting with customers to help them succeed.

Having independent and chain customers in nearly all fifty states, we have the advantage of seeing what is and isn't working at the best and worst coffee houses and drive-thrus across America. Whether you choose Dillanos, or another roaster, make sure they are a good match for you, with the vision and resources to serve as a barista training and business development partner.

Your continuing investment in coffee education should

always be a top priority. Your commitment helps to constantly infuse coffee passion and professionalism in all of your baristas. There is no one size fits all barista training program. While we have endless examples of owner training, ranging from spending six months as a trainee to spending less than a week, we recommend you identify your priorities and what works best for you, then capitalize on the many training opportunities the industry has to offer.

TODAY'S ACTION:

Contact your roaster to gain a clear understanding of what coffee education and barista training support they will provide on an ongoing basis.

Day 13: Motivate Your Team

Now that you have the right staff on board, fully trained, and immersed in the specialty coffee industry, it's time to keep them engaged and excited. Motivation is a broad subject, but when it comes to perfecting the team dynamic, consider these questions:

- Are you demonstrating a culture of pride in your brand?
- Do you have clearly defined job descriptions and systems of accountability?
- Do you provide staff recognition and incentives?
- Is your staff authorized to give refunds, or free product when necessary to resolve customer issues?
- Do your employees regularly show up for work late, without warning?
- Do they gossip and complain about each other and management/owners?
- Do they assume you make so much money that you're being stingy with the hourly pay you're giving them?

It's easy to fall into an adversarial relationship with your staff, but the cause of this dynamic isn't so much about your staff as it is about you. You hold all the cards when it comes to creating a symbiotic relationship with your team. The secret to strong leadership is being vulnerable and open.

Objective number one for vulnerability is for your team to get to know you personally. You need to make it a point to know them beyond their work duties. Be open to sharing concerns, frustrations, or even just personal updates. They need to know you're eager to know more about them as a person, not just as an employee. Consider being available during the off-peak times, like between the hours of two and four in the afternoon. Being on-call during a set time promotes camaraderie that will lead to your team exceeding job requirements. Meeting with them when there are no customers in the café allows you to actively listen to their concerns and ideas to increase business.

It is also beneficial to let your staff understand your baseline goals and numbers. Do they understand your average ticket price goals? Do you set and monitor ambitious and attainable weekly average ticket objectives? Do your baristas suggestively sell your highest margin drinks? Do they know how to promote food add-ons? Do they recognize the cost of goods percentages you need to hit this month? The more you share, the more your staff will take personal ownership and pride in your business. The more involved your team is in understanding your goals, the more involved they'll be in helping you attain them. They will care about things like wasting ingredients, giving away free drinks to their friends, and seeing another employee steal from the till. When every member of your staff is focusing on ways to decrease your expenses, they're now thinking and caring like owners.

Of course, with the added responsibility of knowledge must come the added benefit of rewards. Celebrate together as your business reaches set milestones. The more information you make transparent with your whole team, the more they'll look at your business as their business. With these adjustments, you can eliminate an "us against them" mentality.

Always give clear direction and set performance expectations. Direction and overall performance monitoring has to come from the owner if the team is going to live up to your expectations. Direction needs to be clear from the start, consistent with each staff member, and must come from you. One of the leading causes of demotivation is lack of specific direction. When direction and brand differentiation is ambiguous, it's easy to just put forth minimal effort because there are no set standards of excellence. If you are not completely clear with your staff about your SBI and what success looks like, how can they meet or exceed your goals? Clarity facilitates exceptional work.

One of the most effective techniques for motivating your team is providing incentives. Have you ever explained to your team what one new, regularly tipping customer can do for their annual income? How about just ten regular tipping customers? Assuming they all tip $1 per transaction, that's about $2,500 extra per year, from just 10 customers. Teach your team that the more they increase the company average ticket, the higher their average tip will be per transaction.

"How do we increase their average ticket?" they ask. Strategic add on sales. It's easy to do when the proper motivation is implemented. There are, of course, the basic add-on options: offer the larger drink size first, ask about adding an extra shot, and promote higher margin drinks. The up-sell that scares baristas the most is "the food question." However, it's usually the fastest way to increase each transaction total. If done properly, it's easy to create an option that helps your bottom line, your baristas' tips, and most importantly, is appreciated by your customers. Teach your employees not to use rote language like, "Would you like anything else?" or "Will that be all?" Rather, use specific examples like, "Can I get you a blueberry muffin with that?" The more specific the add-on suggestion, the less likely it is to be ignored. Even if the specific suggestion isn't taken, the customer is more likely to look at another food display item, rather than just passing over the "anything else" comment.

Finally, the most important motivator for your staff is personal recognition. Recognition is such a powerful motivator. As easy as a genuine compliment is to give, it's often the most overlooked tactic for encouraging team members. Recognition needs to be sincere, specific, and publicly announced. Saying the words, "Great job today" falls flat without any specific reason for the compliment. Just like the customer is likely to pass over your barista offering them "anything else," your team will tend to dismiss anything that isn't completely sincere and specific. One of the best ways to recognize staff for specific accomplishments is to hand out awards in your regular staff meetings. It's easy to create a uniquely branded "thank you" ribbon that you can hand out to your employees, or that employees can give to one another. If you don't meet as often as you'd like, why not post a random thank you note to your barista on the wall for them to find? They will take pride in having other baristas see them be recognized by the shift manager or owner.

TODAY'S ACTION:

Make sure you're updating your goals every week. Post the reward that everyone will gain at the end of the goal period. Your team needs to know that you're passionate about meeting their needs and the company's goals.

Day 14: Fewer, Better, and Unique Menu Options

Simplify and minimize your coffee, breakfast, lunch, and snack menu. At the same time, demand perfect drink preparation while dramatically improving originality in one or two main signature food selections. Starbucks' food to beverage ratio is about 80 percent beverage and 20 percent food. This proper balance of food and coffee offerings ensures your business is interpreted as a true coffee house, not as a restaurant. As you know, the best margin is in beverages. Starbucks profits are built on high margin specialty coffee drinks.

Regardless of how engaging your baristas become in making menu suggestions to your customers, it is ultimately your menu that is the prime driver of your average customer ticket. You already know how critical a menu is in a restaurant. Independent and chain restaurants around the country are feverishly revising their menus. Pounded by the recession, they are hoping that some magic combination of prices, adjectives, fonts, type sizes, and appetizing professional photography will coax diners into spending a little more money.

The use of menu engineers and consultants is exploding in

the casual dining arena and among national chains. Owners are tapping into a growing body of menu research, and the science of menu pricing and offerings, hoping the way to the diner's heart is through not only the stomach, but the subconscious association with appeal and quality. Some chains, like Starbucks Reserve cafes, are experimenting with taking pricing off their menus. Like all advertising, menus contain plenty of subliminal messages about your brand.

Successful coffee houses are thriving, as they are rapidly simplifying their menus with exceptional coffees and a few signature food offerings. The coffee house menu is of equal importance to sales and the overall brand image. Your menu can be crucial in the battle of making your customers happier—or losing them. You should always be looking at your menu for more than just pricing changes. Too many owners worry if they change their pricing, or drop some menu listings, they will anger and even lose some customers. Your menu should always be subject to change with trends and new ideas you create to entice customers. Your menu goes to the very heart of your SBI.

While recognizing the critical value of your menu, try not to let your creativity go wild. Creating your menu with a heavy brand design format brings too much of the creative process into menu design. Keep it authentic and simple.

To achieve the best results, try putting yourself in your customer's place and design a menu that is inviting and easy to read, with a large enough font to encourage customers to actually read it. Your baristas will tell you most of your customers walk through your door knowing exactly what they are going to order, unless your short, eye-attracting menu draws their attention. Encourage your baristas to have customers at least glance at the menu as they make suggestions.

You already know it is important to personalize every visit to your coffee house by knowing your customers by name and their favorite beverages. Yet, it is your menu first, then your baristas making new suggestions that will increase your average ticket. Study what today's most successful coffee houses do when it comes to their menu design and offerings. You'll find the most successful examples make their menus simple, enjoyable, and readable, only providing enough categorical information to ensure the menu doesn't become a sea of words. The font size test we like to use is the "three customers deep" rule. Stand back from your service counter as though you have two people in line in front of you. Are you squinting to read the menu? Is it organized with drink and food categories that you can comfortably scan in 30 seconds or less?

Today's best menu strategy is this: less is more. The best way to learn how to create a contemporary coffee house menu today is to visit the most hip and popular coffee houses. If you are in a smaller town with only struggling independent coffee houses surrounded by major coffee chains, you need to travel to Los Angeles, Seattle, Portland, Chicago, Atlanta, or New York to see what is most relevant to customers today in menu design.

Coffee house owners were forced to add new "pillars of profit" with full breakfast and lunch menu offerings to survive the 2008/2009 economic meltdown. As the economy has eased back to a new normal, the best coffee houses have turned to an over-simplified menu. They focus on fewer, better, and unique menu offerings. Trying to sell all things to all people makes you master of none. Never make major decisions based on what a minority of your customers "require" you to offer. Your menu is only one of the reasons you have built a loyal customer base. Uncompromising quality in products and perfect preparation should be the driving force in your menu decisions. We can't stress enough that you need to have every one of your baristas taste everything you list on your menu. Have them pick their personal favorites. This is critical to realizing maximum ticket averages. It also encourages engaging customer conversation.

Research reveals that at least 25 percent of your daily customers ask the barista what they recommend. When your barista genuinely tells the customer their favorite drink or food offering, be assured more often than not, your customers will act on the suggestion.

Some of America's most financially successful coffee houses have done away with wall menu boards altogether. While menu approaches, like interior design, run in trends that are always changing, some former niche hipster coffee house chains going mainstream are using clipboards with a fresh sheet of which coffees are being offered that day. There is no reference to a food menu. This allows flexible options and pricing. Regardless of what menu offering and design you select, use "less is more" as your guide. You will maximize your customer ticket average while defining your café as only serving the best, not the most.

TODAY'S ACTION:

Simplify your menu. Look at every menu offering through your customer's eyes. Stand back from the service counter, three customers deep. Can you select your choice from the menu in less than 30 seconds? Study your menu, while on a mission to eliminate and reduce.

Set up a schedule to have every staff member taste everything you serve. Add suggestive selling of barista favorites to your barista job requirements.

Day 15: Be Unique Within Your Category

Today's American coffee houses and drive-thrus fall within three general categories: independent craft, independent classic, and corporate owned and franchise chains. Your mission is to first understand each category. Recognize the best practices within each as you create your own unique coffee house brand and customer experience.

Independent Craft Coffee Houses

With the majority of today's craft coffee houses, pictures of drinks and pairings are an absolute no-no for their "back to basics and authenticity" SBI. Once considered "niche" independent coffee houses, the skyrocketing success of these quality-above-all cafes has had a direct negative financial impact on classic coffee houses that haven't adapted to the maturing tastes and consistent coffee quality expectations of their customers. When craft coffee houses hit it big, there quickly became a culture of more experienced espresso drinkers. By 2010, mainstream America was seeking out these new, unique places.

What you will often find replacing origin and roasting photos on the walls are chalkboard hand-drawn sketches. It is common to see drawings of manual brew equipment and techniques, farm to cup story drawings with captions, and maps of coffee regions of the world. The collective intended effect of these coffee-centric visuals is to create a more authentic grass roots tribute, and to contribute to customer education about specialty coffee through visual storytelling.

While it could be expected, today very few retail craft coffee brands promote their commitment to environmental protection and community causes. Early craft coffee house brand positioning heavily promoted farm direct relationships and fair farmer pay. Customers now assume craft coffee house owners are committed to environmental and humanitarian causes.

As of this writing, many craft coffee houses have no wall menu. They create a type only "fresh sheet." The ever changing "fresh sheet" highlights single origins, and rare, exotic micro-lots. With few exceptions, food takes a distant second place in attention to their laser focus on coffee. Consistency in providing customers with exceptional blends and single origin coffees perfectly prepared has allowed for little customer concern with industry high menu pricing.

Specialty coffee represents 51 percent of coffee consumed daily by Americans of all ages. Over 40 percent of 18-24 year olds drink specialty coffee daily, up from 31 percent in 2010. That number is continuing to rise. According to a National Coffee Association survey, the 18 to 24 year old demographic preference for specialty coffee increased by 400 percent from the year 2000 to the year 2010. This target customer is golden for the zealot coffee retailers and roasters. The best craft coffee houses perfectly align with the Y generation's requirement for brand authenticity. Ironically, this youth target market has never had less discretionary income, but has never spent more for a coffee. Specialty coffee has replaced soft drinks as the beverage of choice. The unassuming and slogan-free branding of independently owned Craft coffee houses has proliferated and profited since 2010 like no period before. The most foundational commonality of craft retailers is their focus on sourcing and serving exceptional coffees.

The craft coffee house barista training process can take up to three months before the new staff member is set free to prepare drinks without oversight. It begins with required reading on all things coffee, from history to the latest trends. There is also in-depth training on all coffees the café serves before equipment and preparation training. Every barista is required to master latte art to ensure perfection in taste and presentation.

Independent Classic Coffee Houses and Drive-Thrus

When the economy took a nose dive in 2008, many classic coffee houses added ambitious breakfast and lunch offerings to ensure a better than break-even year. Cost of goods skyrocketed as bottom line profit continued to be a challenge. "You can't make it on coffee alone," was the mantra adopted by owners everywhere. This broad demographic continues to place the greatest value on friendliness, a comfortable atmosphere, and consistency in beverage preparation. Barista training usually averages around 20 hours.

Many classic coffee house customers are maturing in their appreciation of exceptional blends and single origin coffees. Recognizing the demand and profit opportunities in serving single origin coffees, many classic coffee houses have added a "slow bar" pour over option. A growing number of classic coffee house owners are recognizing that their coffee quality is as important as controlling their cost of goods. The best and most profitable classic coffee house and drive thru owners are having their baristas serve a better than average specialty coffee. Thematic signature and seasonal mochas and lattes are featured in alluring professional photography on café menus and exterior drive thru menus.

A great example of using walls effectively can be found at Gregory's Coffee coffee houses in Manhattan, New York. At this writing, all ten Gregory's Coffee locations have slight differences to represent changing design trends and local neighborhood ambience. One of Gregory's walls is 12-feet high, created from raw reclaimed wood that runs all the way from floor to ceiling. Subtly stamped on the wood is Gregory's SBI mantra: "We See Coffee Differently." This brand positioning coffee house theme is authentic in the founder's deep understanding and commitment to being a classic coffee house with craft elements.

At many of today's classic coffee houses, baristas are wearing thematic colors and branded shirts and aprons. The intent behind these appearance standards is to comfort the customers, and assure them of standards in quality preparation and brand consistency. More progressive classic coffee houses have stopped requiring uniforms, but still have strict barista appearance standards.

A strategically placed photograph on the menu in today's classic coffee house can pay high dividends. After years of resisting Dillanos' recommendation that well-placed professionally photographed drink and food pairings would boost average ticket sales, Woods founder, Wes Herman decided to test our recommendation. He placed a professionally photographed picture pairing a caramel macchiato with a slice of his slow selling pumpkin bread in the middle of his wall menu boards. He listed no price, just identified the pairing as a fall menu suggestion. The wood cutting board background was simple, with the drink and pumpkin bread slice as inviting as a photo you would see on the cover of Food & Wine Magazine. Before putting up the photo, Woods' white chocolate raspberry scone outsold all of his other dessert offerings, three to one. It was the signature baked good which Woods' own bakery made fresh daily. Once the photo was placed between the menu boxes, pumpkin bread sales skyrocketed in demand, soon equal to his white raspberry scone sales. The scone sales didn't go down, but the pumpkin bread quickly became its equal in customer preference, all without the baristas doing any more than taking customer orders.

Woods classic coffee houses are a great example of using photography strategically and sparingly to increase average ticket sales. While every new Woods cafe progresses in interior design trends, this family owned and operated classic chain has seen a direct bottom line benefit from the strategic use of photography.

Corporate and Franchise Chains

Starbucks created and defined the retail specialty coffee house in America for the industry's first twenty years of existence. In Howard Shultz's book, Pour Your Heart Into It, he states that his mission was to create a consistent customer experience in an inviting and comfortable environment. He envisioned and quickly made Starbucks a customer's "third place." There was home, work, and your local Starbucks. By the mid 1990s Starbucks and a handful of franchise chains replaced the local bar for social and business gatherings.

The cookie cutter look for coffee houses across America blurred the lines of differentiation with all competing brands. Chains like Coffee Bean & Tea Leaf, Peet's, Caribou, and Tully's have followed Starbucks model of investing in a consistent design and customer experience. They have all struggled to create any brand differentiation that made them a viable alternative to the exploding growth of Starbucks. Little needs to be said about corporate and franchise coffee houses' extensive use of menu photography to promote mochas, lattes, and seasonal favorites.

By 2010, most franchises were failing, and even Starbucks was losing its niche as a prestigious brand. Classic coffee houses, also following the cookie cutter interior design lead from major chains were seeing a significant shift in customer loyalty based on the powerful influence of eclectic craft coffee houses. Howard Shultz could see where the future was going. In his return to the role of president and Chief Executive Officer in 2008, he declared at his annual stockholders meeting that Starbucks was "going back to basics." Influenced and pressured by the success of Stumptown and other rising craft coffee retailers, he introduced the Shared Planet coffee houses. He started shifting from the cookie cutter look to a more "authentic" and eclectic interior design look. His first Shared Planet coffee house in Seattle's Pioneer Square had a bean bag covered wall, and reclaimed furniture and counter finishes. At the same time, Starbucks introduced single cup preparation to mainstream America with their purchase of the Clover single cup preparation system.

In December of 2013, as the Shared Planet look and "save the planet" brand positioning evolved, Starbucks unveiled the first Starbucks Reserve coffee house as the chain's primary growth strategy for the next five years in North America. Starbucks Reserve coffee houses are far closer in design and atmosphere to a trendy craft coffee house than to the cookie cutter Starbucks look of the past.

There is little photography on the menu. The only visuals have the appearance of hand drawn coffee geography, seed-to-cup sketches, and freestanding chalk drawings of featured seasonal drinks. Prices are higher, with the theme, "rare and exotic coffees." There are no prices listed. In early 2014, Starbucks retained interior designers in a multitude countries to design cafes that fully embrace the local ambience of the neighborhood and community of each location. With so many locations, the result of this attempt to move closer to the classic coffee house's strategy of building a relationship with each customer has been inconsistent. Starbucks and other franchise and corporate owned coffee houses are still transactional and largely impersonal in taking customer orders. Baristas still wear uniforms.

The stabilization of the economy, and maturing customer expectations of exceptional coffee and perfect preparation has resulted in the acceleration of the Starbucks Reserve Coffee House concept. These locations represent the chain's vision of effectively competing with encroaching craft and classic coffee houses.

TODAY'S ACTION:

Go to a nearby independent classic, independent craft, and Starbucks or other franchise coffee house. Having read this book so far, you should be able to better identify their strengths and weaknesses in branding, barista coffee knowledge, and customer service. Seek out what each segment is doing best, and incorporate their greatest strengths in creating your own SBI.

Day 16: Café Layout and Design

Would you wear the same clothes you did five years ago? Once your major investment is made in designing your coffee house or drive-thru, your creativity can easily and understandably go on auto pilot. Based on the average length of design trends, your color scheme, wall hangings, and furniture can all too quickly be as outdated as out of fashion clothes.

As you envision the way a new café space is going to look, imagine pieces like your espresso machine and a custom designed bar. Further down the investment list is the collection of chairs and tables at which your customers will make themselves comfortable. Chairs and tables are far too undervalued in the ambience and SBI most coffee house owners envision.

If your furniture is contemporary, like today's industrial chic with wood accents, but isn't ergonomically comfortable, you have allowed comfort to come a distant second to a trendy look. If your furniture is comfortable, inviting, and varied to be conducive to both brief and long conversations, you have accomplished the first step in successfully selecting your furnishings.

The idea is to connect with customers through all their senses, so décor and furniture play an integral role. When your customers first walk in your doors, your mission is to get them to connect with the look, then the smell of fresh ground coffee, as they listen to music set at the perfect volume. Far too often, too little is invested in proper ceiling acoustics to allow easy conversation in a busy coffee house. Your chairs, tables, and other furniture go a long way toward establishing the desired ambience. As an owner, you may be tempted to choose pieces that are extensions of your own home design and living or family room taste. Get into that trap and you have taken Howard Schultz's "third place" idea too far. Furniture is a key element of holistic branding; it must be an extension of your SBI.

Where can you place your furniture for maximum function in your café? How do you decide what types of tables, chairs, flooring, and wall surfaces will be relevant for the next three to five years? Knowing the answers to these questions can help you design and furnish your café in the way that most efficiently communicates your SBI, and in turn, instantly resonates with your customers.

Where to Place It

While the look of your furniture plays a huge role in your café's ambience, the number of seats and where they're placed also contributes to the overall feel and to your profits. Tom Palm, President of Design & Layout Services, says a general layout rule is that a café should take its total square footage and divide it in half. Half of the space goes to backroom, kitchen, storage, service counters, and restrooms. Palm says you should then divide the remaining square footage by 20, resulting in the number of seats. For example, a 2,000-square-foot space will have 1,000 square feet for seating, with a total of 50 seats.

Gone are the days of couches and loveseats. They are an inefficient use of space and make your coffee house look dated. People rarely share a couch with someone they don't know, so often one person may be taking up seating space for three.

Have two to four comfortably cushioned chairs to soften the room and add many standard height tables for seating, accented by high-top tables with stools.

If the space and views outside accommodate it, add counters with stools at the windows with an electric outlet for every seat. Free Wi-Fi is a must and comes with an added demand for easy access to charging smart phones, tablets, or laptops. How should seating be arranged? Palm says unique placement is a hallmark of high-end coffee houses. You don't want just a collection of standard square tables with four seats at them. This looks like a banquet center, not an engaging coffee house. You want a variety of individual chairs and tables of different sizes and shapes that can be moved around to accommodate parties of different sizes.

When choosing furniture, consider both contemporary trends and the taste and preferences of your target customer base. Your interior design is all about creating an inviting space where your customer feels comfortable. Set aside funds for furniture updates every so often. If you don't discipline yourself to have a budget to update your decor, you won't have the resources to proactively compete.

Contemporary Minimalism

While contemporary coffee house design is a moving target with a growing focus on local interior accents, the mainstream trend today is contemporary minimalism.

Today's trend-leading coffee houses are heavily influenced by commercial and high-end home kitchen design. Walls are varied with different textures. Furniture has a hint of industrial chic metal for stools and chairs, a clean, polished, metalwork look, complemented by finished, lighter, multi-colored wood walls, and natural wood tables provide warm contrast to a stark minimalism. Wood accents are sometimes covered in a high polish, juxtaposed by raw, untreated pieces, all within the same structure. Lighting is eclectic and contemporary. Walls are often bare, or have sparsely placed pictures or drawings.

Service counter tops have moved from reclaimed facings, wood, and granite, to white marble and quartz. The clean and minimalized white look, boldly brought to market by Apple retail stores, has had a contributing influence on many trend-setting coffee houses today.

The aforementioned trend is a simplified, broad brush look at current popular interior designs that can be found in major coffee houses in cities and rural areas across the nation, and of course, other designs are constantly emerging. Looking forward under Howard Schultz's watch, Starbucks is now aggressively investing in original design conceptualization, grounded in making each coffee house as original as where it is located. Local territorialism is taking the place of nationalism in design trends. Communities are doing whatever they can to support local businesses when given the option, so long as quality and service aren't compromised. Take advantage of this by accenting your café with neighborhood design ambience.

TODAY'S ACTION:

Focus on commercial, basic, and minimalized contemporary kitchen design today by doing Internet research. Seek out today's hottest coffee houses on www.sprudge.com. Start envisioning the wall colors and varied textures as well as the styles of furniture and lighting that will contribute to your SBI. Continually study current and changing interior design trends, while making sure to stay true to your SBI, and not just echo others with a "me too" strategy.

Day 17: Sustainability and Transparency

What does sustainability and transparency mean for coffee houses today, and for your customers? What is coffee house sustainability? There are two components. The first is your roaster's commitment, and the second is your coffee house's commitment.

Your roaster's purchasing practices are fundamental in supporting the environmental and economic needs of the global coffee community. Coffee is grown between the tropics of Cancer and Capricorn, where 70 percent of the poorest people on earth struggle to make a living to support themselves and their families. Choosing to sell organic, Fair Trade, farm direct, or relationship-based coffee provides maximum benefit to the farmer, the land, and the wildlife on the land where the coffee is grown. Individually and collectively, these practices represent a genuine commitment to sustainability.

The second component is your coffee house's commitment. Current research reveals that any retailer gains quicker and deeper loyalty from a broad spectrum of customers by displaying a commitment to the greater good now that "sustainability" has gone mainstream in America. Sustainability has been a buzzword in the food industry since 2005, as evidenced by giant food service distributors like Sysco and U.S. Foods mandating that their buyers give preference to suppliers committed to sustainability. This socially conscious focus is driven by customers, including state colleges and universities who themselves are focusing more every day on aligning with vendors deeply committed to sustainability.

The general public is hungry to learn more about the path their food or drink has taken and how their choices impact the earth. The huge public groundswell of interest in organic and healthy foods has resulted in chains like Whole Foods flourishing in the grocery category. By comparison, most other national grocery chains are either merging or struggling as rising food costs force them into price wars, blurring or shattering their brand positioning.

The challenge for you as a coffee house owner is focusing on sustainability with your customers in such a way that it doesn't feel like your baristas are lecturing them on the virtues of your food and beverage sourcing practices. The answer to whether or not your customers care about your roaster's commitment to sustainability is easily answered in the success other large brands, such as Starbucks, have seen with highlighting sustainability. Starbucks has made its commitment to the earth and humanity a central talking point. As pointed out earlier, "Starbucks is bigger than coffee." Ethical sourcing and environmental stewardship are hallmarks of the brand's SBI. While most Starbucks baristas have little knowledge and rarely speak on the topic, their core values and brochures are very clear about aligning the brand with its recognized social and environmental responsibilities.

Today, no retail industry is more connected to sustainability and authenticity than the specialty coffee industry, so how do you incorporate sustainability into your SBI? Start by aligning with a roaster who values ethical and environmentally sensitive sourcing. Their story is your story, as the buyer of your beans. As an owner, explore the opportunity to accompany your roaster on an origin trip. Find a worthy cause connected to your roaster, or the coffee industry, and make it your own.

As you enter into single-cup brewing, each offering will help your customers appreciate single-origins, the story of the coffee, and growing practices more every day. Every one of your baristas should be able to tell the story of your connection to the farm or producer, or something else unique about the coffee in addition to describing basic flavor notes. Armed with coffee confidence, your baristas will be able to create a deeper customer appreciation for the coffees you serve.

Your baristas have the power to improve the taste, and begin justifying a higher price, even before the customers taste the coffee. Imagine your barista explaining, "The Brazil coffee in your macchiato will perfectly enhance the flavor of the sweet milk." Nobody likes a lecture. Everybody loves a good story.

Use your roaster's website, your own site, and other sources of coffee education without beating your customers over the head with dry, generic coffee information. Consider telling some of the story with photographs of you, or your lead trainer at origin. Sustainability doesn't have to be your SBI's main focus, but it should be included via weekly posts on your website and regularly scheduled customer tastings. Over time, with your staff's subtle encouragement, your customers will seek out more and more knowledge about their favorite coffees.

TODAY'S ACTION:

Go to your roaster's website and explore the depth of their commitment to ethical sourcing and environmental stewardship. Call your roaster and schedule a meeting to discuss how your coffee house can make their commitment part of your own story. Draft a plan of how you are going to engage your staff and customers in your commitment to sustainability in an authentic and engaging way.

Day 18: Keep it Social

Social media is no longer something a single or multi-location coffee house owner can put on the back burner. Effective use of social media can foster huge growth in awareness and customers, but only if it is done right. A general notion of fun and interesting engagement needs to be the underlying driver for all your social media efforts. Taking the time and investment to develop and execute a high quality social media strategy can help your business reach new levels of success.

Coffee houses that connect frequently with their customers are dramatically increasing a deeper level of customer relationships and engagement. There are a handful of coffee house owners recognizing that, unlike marketing that has come before, social media is a two-way street.

The rules of customer engagement are also entirely different than in traditional advertising. A stronger connection is crucial to building word-of-mouth business. A transactional attitude in specialty coffee will never breed brand loyalty. Fostering loyalty requires a collaborative, life-long relationship with your brand by exceeding expectations at nearly all points of contact.

The list below gives you a basic action plan outlining key, prioritized concerns.

- It all starts with defining your SBI, then building a social media program around it.
- Independent coffee houses have a huge opportunity to focus on local needs. Don't just focus on the specialty coffee industry with coffee-centric education and information. Focus on a variety of subjects that would be of interest to your customers.
- When using social media, break your customer base into segments. Stay-at-home moms may have different interests or preferences than business people looking for a place to meet. What does each target customer group care about most?
- Social media is about listening to your customers, not just pushing your brand, culture, and menu offerings down the audience's throat. Consider what you personally enjoy seeing on social media when determining what your business should post.
- Promotional content, including menu offerings and special drink coupons, should not take up the majority of your posts. The mission of your website homepage is to get your visitors to what they care about most as quickly as possible. Your potential customers will likely Google "best coffee house," so investing in search engine optimization may be beneficial.

When creating your social media plan, think back to that well-worn saying, "Trust takes a lifetime to build and a moment to lose." The other truth in marketing is that content is king. This statement has begun ringing even more true in the digital age. Your customers expect a personalized experience. You have a website, Facebook page, and possibly a blog or Twitter account, but there's one catch. You don't have time to post fun, educational, and business differentiating copy, pictures, and video every week.

Here is our answer to your marketing dilemma.

- Source your most social media-savvy barista.
- Pay them a premium hourly wage to work an hour or more, five days a week in exploring and posting on social media.
- Have them scan Yelp and other reviewing sites daily to ensure you are getting and replying to real-time customer compliments and complaints.
- This dedicated social media staff member can also oversee in coming emails from customers.
- On a near daily basis, they should be posting content on appropriate platforms such as Facebook, Twitter, and Instagram.

Social media has become a core component of accelerating word of mouth about your coffee house. About 46 percent of online users count on social media to make purchasing decisions. Effectively using social media can help you find new customers and maintain current customer relationships. Social media will also help you build awareness, acceptance, and repeat business faster than traditional media has ever been able to accomplish at a fraction of the cost.

Clarify Goals and Regularly Strategize with Your Staff

Determine and write down your short and long term objectives for social media in your business plan. Address what you will invest in terms of time and money. Once you establish specific social media goals, you can come up with key metrics in order to keep an eye on progress in a concrete way. You can then use this as a roadmap in creating promotional strategies to achieve the goals you set.

When creating your social media strategy, determine how it

fits into targeting existing and potential customers. Develop a clear plan for the use of social media to increase your daily customer count and average ticket. This will help keep your social media program focused on the big picture.

Use the Right Social Networks for the Specialty Coffee Business

While social media is constantly changing, at this writing, Facebook, Instagram, and Twitter are probably the most effective platforms for coffee houses. Stay close to the ever changing trends and options in social media.

As an owner, think beyond your local community outreach in building your SBI. You have an opportunity to be recognized on a national level via the specialty coffee industry's own media (i.e. www.sprudge.com, Fresh Cup and Barista magazines' print and digital magazines). The specialty coffee industry media is constantly seeking out coffee house brands with unique SBIs, as well as unique community and coffee-centric events and activities. Add these niche networks to your social media plan.

Focus on ROI

In order to keep track of the effectiveness of your social media, understanding return on investment is a must. Don't just look at the vanity metrics, such as followers and "likes." Measure activity, engagement, reach, and customer sourcing. Have cards at your condiment bar that ask customers to check off where they heard about your coffee house.

Become an Active Part of the Conversation

An active social media presence done right means people will be talking about your brand. Yelp, Urban Spoon, and other review sites allow you to not only be aware of what people are saying about you, but help you see the strengths and weaknesses of your competition. Seek out both positive and negative comments from customers and non-customers. Use this information on a weekly basis to adjust staff and core practices according to what people like and dislike. Be cautious not to overreact to negative comments, but view these unpleasant reviews as opportunities to win people over. Make the situation right by conversing with the customer on the site on which they left their review. Offer a sincere apology and invite them in for a free drink and a new experience. Conversations on social media are an opportunity to eradicate the disconnect between what you believe your customers think and what they really want. Make listening and quick responsiveness a priority.

Shoot for Quality Rather Than Quantity

The more directly sales-focused posts you feature, the fewer followers you will gain. It is significantly more important to focus on creating and posting fun and high quality content. Customers will actually want to pay attention and share this content, driving more traffic. As part of this content focus, set up a blog of your own, and be a guest blogger on select industry sites. Blog content should tell a short story and be relevant and beneficial to all who read it.

Infusing character into your social media presence is extremely valuable. This often includes humor and wit. An inspirational and emotional voice is also effective. When you find what works well with your followers, stick with it. By showing the playful side of your business, and your authentic commitment to quality, you'll deliver the perfect combination to become a person's favorite coffee house. Consistency in brand personality (SBI) is crucial to social media. Be consistent in your activity, style of originality, and information.

Be Visual

Share pictures and videos that are fun, inspiring, and pertinent to the specialty coffee industry. One study indicates that image posts on Facebook garner 53 percent more likes and 94 percent more comments than posts with only links or text. Clearly, adding a visual dimension to the digital expression of your SBI can make a huge difference.

TODAY'S ACTION:

Determine if you or someone on your staff will serve as your social media leader. Devise an action plan for you and your staff to "get in the game" and blast every effort through social media channels as an ongoing brand building strategy.

Day 19: Coffee with a Cause

No retail industry is more dedicated to social responsibility than the retail coffee business. Common sense dictates that having a good reputation in your neighborhood and community is integral to customer loyalty to your brand. While there are a handful of highly successful coffee-centric cafes singularly dedicated to preparing the perfect cup from a perfect coffee, you will build a long lasting and loyal customer base by committing time, focus, and marketing dollars to global coffee and community causes. Your causes are most dramatically reflected in your coffee house, website, and social media. Actively engaging in causes beyond your own profit helps define the soul of your brand. Your staff and customers will gain a deeper pride in your brand when your commitment isn't a shallow marketing ploy, but runs deep and personal.

Every coffee house claims its mission is to serve its community. The reality is, most owners and baristas confine being active in the community to providing a welcoming place for locals to enjoy an exceptional cup of coffee. In truth, active personal participation in community causes by your business is a major driver in your brand power. Sharing these activities via social media promotes the overall perception of your business. The importance of corporate social responsibility (CSR) has a profound impact on customer purchase behavior and loyalty. CoreBrand, a national research firm, tracks how purchase behavior is tied to the level of a Fortune 500 company's CSR every year. Food and beverage manufacturers rank highest in association of brand equity with level of commitment to social causes.

Limit Your Causes

Pick only one or two causes. As the owner, you need to get involved, showing your commitment to every member of your staff in order to draw their enthusiasm. Coffee with a cause isn't just an add-on to a marketing strategy. It has to be heartfelt and believable that you, as the owner, and your staff are serving beyond your own self-interest. CoreBrand summarizes CSR as follows: "It contributes to the total brand experience, builds trust, familiarity and favorability. It improves key brand attributes, and it contributes measurably to brand equity value."

Be committed to only one or two causes. This focus allows you to make a difference that resonates through your community. Today's coffee house is all about heart, starting with you. At our company, Dillanos, we have paid for every employee to sponsor a child in a coffee-growing country through Child Fund International since the mid-nineties. Recently, the non-profit organization's Chief Executive Officer, Anne Goddard, came to see us and said she knows of no other company in America that sponsors a child for every employee. This clear commitment to a cause shows what we value. For us, Child Fund makes sense; we care deeply about family and helping people.

TODAY'S ACTION:

Narrow down the causes your business currently supports with time, coffee, or money. The most important consideration in "going limited and deep" is to choose no more than two causes that have deep personal connection to you, and soon after, your staff.

Day 20: Create Your Own Specific Brand Image (SBI)

As addressed in our prologue, the best place to start your branding adventure is with the second reading of this book. Your own SBI should start taking form as you read and jot down ideas on the action day suggestions.

There is so much more involved in what marketing professionals and business owners casually call branding, that we decided we had to develop a guide to crafting your SBI. Does your own Specific Brand Image still sound abstract at this stage of reading this book? Not if you get your holistic branding glasses in focus. You will read over and over in different marketing books that branding is all encompassing.

As a business leader, or owner, first and foremost, you are central to your brand. Have you applied your brand to how you dress, walk and talk to your staff and customers? You are the living manifestation of your brand.

The music played in your café should be the same music your primary customers would enjoy, set at a volume that contributes to ambience, but doesn't interfere with quiet conversation. Even the cleanliness of your café and bathroom is integral to your SBI, exemplifying that everything associated with your business should be purposeful.

By now you should be internalizing and making "branding is everything, and everything is branding" your mantra. People don't just buy products and services. They buy into an identity represented by where they shop, where they eat, and their highly personalized choice of coffee houses or drive-thrus.

Your brand is the powerful selling tool you must first understand, then create, control, and evolve. Once you step into the world of holistic branding, your brand will take on a meaning to your customers far greater than the sum of its parts.

The word brand literally means "to burn." This is a perfect description of what you need to accomplish: burning your brand into your customer's mind. The soul of your brand is built on your SBI. Make the vision yours.

Criteria to Develop A Unique SBI

- There must be clearly distinguishable differences from your competition.
- Make it believable.
- Make it sustainable.
- Strategically differentiate enough from your competition to create a clear SBI.
- Be consistent with every aspect of your SBI by reflecting it in your mission statement and core values.
- You and your staff need to be able to state your SBI in 30 seconds.
- Aggressively seek out employee ownership and customer feedback.
- Encourage candid input that keeps your SBI honest in everything you do.

To make the idea of an SBI real, let's look at Dillanos Coffee

Roasters' as an example. More than a national award-winning specialty coffee roaster, Dillanos is a customer business development partner. To ensure our SBI is real, believable, and sustainable, Dillanos has long invested in a seasoned marketing director and full design department for our customers. We created a separate business development department as well. Every business development representative's (BDR) singular responsibility is to provide counsel and tools to measurably contribute to our customer's success. A BDR is assigned to serve the needs and opportunities of every member of the Dillanos customer family, and the BDR's daily mission is to actively help existing customers grow and become more profitable. Our mission statement, supported by actionable core values is: Help People. Make Friends. Have Fun.

To make the concept of an SBI less abstract, stop reading at this stage and go to the coffee house websites listed below.

Durango Joe's—www.durangojoes.com

Durango Joe's Coffee was established in 2004 by Joe Lloyd and his wife LeAnna with a dream of becoming the local and regional coffee house that locals feel is their own.
The family has a legendary history in Durango that is as rich and memorable as the coffee they serve. Once Joe embraced his roots in the transient resort community, he had struck gold for a unique SBI.
Joe's grandfather, Durango's own Doctor Leo Lloyd, served the Durango community for over 40 years in family medicine. Doc Lloyd was beloved for his night and day to-home bedside care. He set the family's "community first" mission in the early 1900s.
Joe's brother , Leo Lloyd III, is known throughout the Four Corners as the go to guy for dangerous search and rescue missions.

He serves as a captain for the Durango Fire Department.

Joe himself is a community leader and local charity advocate. Besides his many coffee origin trips and passionate commitment to continual learning, and serving great coffees, he shares his family's spirit of exceptional service to his community. Joe and his staff genuinely believe that all people are important. When you walk into any of the Durango Joe's locations, it is impossible not to notice the over-the-top customer service and pride in, as they call it, "legendary community" and "legendary coffee."

Gregory's Coffee--www.gregoryscoffee.com

When the Dillanos sales leadership team first met Gregory Zamfotis, founder and co-owner of Gregory's Coffee, he had just closed one of three locations in lower Manhattan. Greg struggled to find his own SBI. With a law degree in hand, and as a natural at branding, Greg soon realized that he was his coffee house's SBI. The tall, lean, dark curly-haired hipster with oversized black-rimmed glasses was immediately recognizable by his signature buttoned-up white shirt and skinny black tie. Greg personified the brand perfectly in his intense passion for studying coffee as diligently as he had studied law. His obsession with specialty coffee knowledge, combined with highly engaging customer service started to catch fire with Manhattan's coffee lovers.

Study how perfectly Greg's sophisticated minimalist logo, a caricature of his face, and website cut through the noise of the competition with a clearly defined SBI. Greg's SBI has become so successful in Manhattan that Fox News created a television news segment titled, "David and Goliath: How to compete with Starbucks." Greg, sitting up straight in his signature glasses with his scuffed wingtip shoes and no socks, was as relaxed as a late night talk show host. Introduced as the "David" in the feature with the huge Starbucks logo behind him, Greg fully captured the essence of his SBI when he was asked what made Gregory's Coffee so different. "Just be yourself," Greg said with a wry smile.

What do Durango Joe's and Gregory's Coffee have in common? They both have an SBI that is as unique as each of them, and an unstoppable passion for exceeding expectations and serving customers consistent, quality products.

TODAY'S ACTION:

Think about whether or not your business has, or will have, a differentiating SBI. At this stage of your first reading of this guide to success, new ideas should be emerging that will significantly differentiate your brand from the competition. Jot down a few first draft ideas.

Day 21: Navigate with a Plan

Now that we have covered all the key ingredients in creating a powerful SBI, you are ready to address the building of a formal business plan. Even if you already have a coffee house, take a couple of steps back and build a business plan. Whether you have been a specialty coffee retailer for six years, or six months, a business plan will better help you define your SBI and improve your bottom line. Don't let the thought scare you. We encourage you to wait until you have finished reading this book a second time before you launch into crafting your business plan on the assigned action day.

You have probably heard the line, "Fail to plan, and you plan to fail." Only a handful of coffee house owners ever write a business/marketing plan, but don't let the idea overwhelm you as a huge burden on your to-do list. You really can write your business plan in a few days if you first write down your refined ideas at the end of each action day in your second reading of this book.

Effective brands rely on a written concept overview to keep the owner and staff focused as your brand and/or enhanced SBI unfolds. Savvy owners are taking advantage of the specialty coffee house rage that continues to sweep the country. Along with capitalizing on the trend, they are also planning for the future.

The standard business plan includes the following table of contents, in this order:

- Executive Summary
- Mission Statement
- Business Differentiation (SBI)
- Business Goals
- Description of the Business
- Current Retail Specialty Coffee Market Snapshot
- Coffee House Competition—Strengths and Weaknesses
- Critical Risks and Challenges
- Marketing Plan
- Operations
- Management
- Financials

Before you sit down to write your business plan, you need to assemble background information about your business. We recommend utilizing the following assumptions in creating your financial plan if you do not already have a location open.

- Cost of goods: 32-35 percent
- Labor: 25 percent
- Occupancy (lease, triple net, utilities): 10 percent
- Owner's compensation: 10 percent
- Marketing: 10 percent

As a general rule, you should be realizing a profit before taxes of 10 to 17 percent. These overly simplified guidelines identify expenses subject to variances by market.

These percentages change based on the vulnerability of rising coffee, milk, food, and paper goods costs. While demanding market-leading quality as your foundational cost of goods guide, always seek out industry averages in the categories where you can control expenses. As noted earlier, keep food around 20 percent or less and beverages around 80 percent or more of your menu to realize maximum profits.

Aside from initial lease negotiations and renegotiations, you can't control monthly occupancy expenses, but you must monitor cost of goods, labor, and marketing.

Invest in a point-of-sale (POS) system that makes single and multi-location ticket averages easy to access, while taking key financial measures and labor needs projections into account.

Set quarterly goals to increase your average ticket, leading to new ways your baristas can better engage in suggestive selling, while increasing their tips and your bottom line.

To further your understanding and assembly of vital information for your business plan, the following provides more detail for some of the previously mentioned business plan table of contents.

Business Description

- The name of your business
- Location
- Your menu
- Pictures (or renderings) of exterior/interior of the building
- Floor plan
- Leasing arrangements
- Architect/contractor estimates for new building

Management Profile:

You are not only the owner, but likely the primary manager. Include a one page resume. If you have, or plan to have a partner, include their brief biography. If you are retaining a consultant, or your roaster provides needed value-added services, include this in your management profile, along with the roaster's website address.

A Statement About the Coffee Industry

Do a quick online search to find the latest industry trends. Include the most current specialty coffee drinker demographics and consumption trends. The Specialty Coffee Association of America website (SCAA.org) will often have relevant industry trend information that you can use for this section.

Major Competitors

From previous action day research, you are ready to call out the key strengths and weaknesses of your specialty coffee competition. While auditing the competition, honestly consider the strengths and weaknesses of your business.

Key Financial Data

The financial section of your business plan requires four documents: A pro forma, a balance sheet, a cash flow statement, and an income statement or P & L. To gather these figures, work with a qualified accountant for guidance.

Owner Compensation Recognition

Pay yourself a salary, and factor it into your overall labor expenses. You are central to your business's operations, whether you serve customers, oversee daily activities, or serve as a "brand ambassador." By accounting for yourself, you'll ensure an income and have a more accurate method of making decisions and forecasting your annual profit.

Executive Summary

Once all the information needed is gathered, write your executive summary. This is the last portion you write, and it is placed at the front of your business plan. It highlights the most important strengths of your business, starting with your Specific Brand Image, followed by key points from your plan's table of contents. It shouldn't be more than one to two pages long.

Business Plan Benefits

Besides being fundamental to creating a unique brand, your business plan serves a multitude of other purposes. It will help you:

- Approach banks, lenders, or investors for financing for your business.
- Expand a single location business, or create the template for more locations.
- Increase your current average customer ticket and bottom line.

TODAY'S ACTION:

Download the book titled, Business Plan in a Day by Rhonda Abrams. This book is very user-friendly. Most how-to books on business plans aren't worth the time they take to read. This book is head and shoulders above all other business plan books. It is the perfect choice for someone who has never written a formal business plan.

Source an accountant with experience in business planning. Start the process of creating a lean action-oriented business plan that shouldn't exceed 10-20 pages.

Over the next several weeks, keep working on your plan, filling in any missing, or vague information. After you have finished all 22 action day notes in your second reading of this book, go back and better refine your SBI. Keep it short and crystal clear.

Day 22: Owner's Playbook

Now that you have brought all the pieces together to launch, or revitalize your business, it is time to create your weekly playbook. Dillanos Business Development Supervisor Chris Buck formerly managed a highly profitable Starbucks location in Washington State. His Monday morning playbook was foundational to staff retention and profits.

Being a team sports fan, Chris decided to use sports metaphors to coach a team with a common vision and mission. Every Monday morning before Starbucks opened, Chris would spend an hour deciding that week's average customer ticket objective by reviewing the past week's hourly and daily sales. He would also look at each barista's average transaction total to particularly focus on those baristas who didn't meet the previous week's sales objectives. From six to ten in the morning, Chris' ultimate mission was to complete 80 transactions every half hour. Chris decided to employ a sales strategy of focusing on one high profit margin item each week. As coach, he chose one food or drink menu item as the singular focus for suggestive selling that week. He consciously kept the goals as simple and memorable as possible. Every barista needed to find ten minutes everyday from their behind the counter routine to walk the café, look around, and clean tables and the floor as needed. As the barista cleaned up the room, another barista would prepare a pastry sample plate or four-ounce, high margin drink tray. The cleaning barista would complete their duties by walking around the coffee house and offering samples to customers. Besides ensuring daily sampling, the strategy reminded baristas of which menu item was being highlighted.

Thanks to every Monday morning's staff huddle, Chris' employees shared in a common daily goal that contributed to a team atmosphere. They also got feedback on what did and didn't work the previous week.

In creating your own playbook, consider including the following sections.

- Daily Focus
  - Examples: Motivation statement for the day, inspirational quote, focus on teamwork, or customer interactions
- Daily Suggestions
  - What drink, or food item are you focusing on selling today?
- Daily Goals
  - Total sales
  - Sales by shift
  - Dollars per transaction
- Daily Staffing
  - Who is working and when
  - Any specific tasks assigned to each team member
- Daily Notes
  - Any incidents out of the ordinary, events being held in your café, shout-outs for exemplary work, or anything else your staff needs to know

Chris set weekly office hours for his staff to share any personal or business ideas or concerns. While Starbucks and the industry average a near 70 percent annual turnover, Chris' nurturing attention, genuine active listening, and empathetic caring contributed to a much lower turnover rate. Before you can gain the kind of loyal staff following Chris achieved as team coach, you need to have the qualities of an inspirational leader.

Melissa and Ray Vandervalk, owners of Red Leaf Organic Coffee in Kelso, Washington, shared a great leadership feedback tool valuable to any business leader. Melissa discovered a leadership staff survey created by Andy Andrews, prolific author of business leadership books. She created a list of qualities and skills based on Andy Andrews' survey, and handed the list out to her baristas. Employees were provided with the opportunity to give feedback by highlighting the five things management did best in yellow and highlighting five areas of opportunity in green. This method inspired honest input from the team. Often, handwriting can easily identify who is making negative comments in staff surveys, so after removing this "threat," employees were more open. Even better, the survey was insightful and dug down to the core of effective leadership.

The survey read as follows.

- Clarity and consistency in verbal and written communication
- Able to set fair boundaries for all staff members
- Willing and able to delegate effectively
- Does not micromanage any department
- Able to assess contributing strengths as well as weaknesses in others.
- Often praise employees outside staff meetings
- Able to present information and tasks in a way that doesn't crowd a person's/group's/organization's mind too much
- Focuses on staff praise more than self praise

- Benevolence and compassion for every employee
- Sets strategic 3 to 5 year vision
- Ability to drive the hammer, if needed
- They don't people please and recognize as much as they please and recognize themselves
- They assign people jobs they are good at and have a genuine desire to do
- They redirect people, attitudes, and situations before they become a problem
- They make a safe environment for people to take initiative and set up guidelines, then get out of the way
- They believe in human potential and see more good things in their staff than they see in themselves
- They raise the bar everyday
- They create measurements to gauge progress
- They know and act quickly when a staff member doesn't fit the culture or job
- They understand the power of writing things down
- They have the ability to slow people down, to think, and to become aware of the moment
- They listen to their intuition and use sound logic
- They don't forget that happiness is important, and acts should be for the betterment of the whole
- They lead responsibly and ethically

After getting the feedback from the Red Leaf staff, Melissa wrote, "It taught me that great leaders have a plan to accomplish something, then they lay it out for everyone involved, so each person knows their part." Melissa found out her biggest issue was micromanaging. "I realized I am always nitpicking and correcting people. They felt like they couldn't do things right. With five people working beside me when we were busiest, I was just putting out fires left and right without taking a breath to oversee staff satisfaction and smooth operations. Even if I felt they knew it, I didn't really show total trust until we implemented a disciplined training program for preparation and customer service. After the survey, I decided it was me that needed to change. For over a month now, our existing and new staff has been provided with the right foundation to learn perfect preparation and customer interaction skills. I am consciously trying to reinforce their roles as part of our proud team. A simple survey really woke me up. In short: vision, planning, asking for cooperation from people who share the same vision, laying out goals, patient training, measuring progress, happiness, and being clear with expectations has had immediate benefits."

Since proactively responding to staff concerns, average ticket and barista tips are higher, and a happier staff is building a more profitable business everyday. It is time for you to create your own playbook.

TODAY'S ACTION:

Before you create your playbook, gain staff input on your role as their coach. Use the questionnaire above with your team. Be open and ready to make whatever personal leadership adjustments are needed to be inspirational and directional. Create and implement your own Monday morning weekly playbook.

Final Word

Whether you have a single coffee house or lead a major franchise chain, every brand needs refreshing to stay relevant. Your savvy customers appreciate investments and improvements made in your physical store, your staff, and your products. You can keep building same-store sales if you show and sustain improvement.

Today's cutting-edge coffee is all about nuance. It tends to be lighter roasted than the darker roasts that first defined specialty coffee in the 1990s. Espresso was, and still is, a classic coffee drink, but various forms of single-cup brewing methods have been revived. The French press, pour over, and vacuum methods are all part of this new wave. The closer attention to manually brewing each coffee in its own unique manner is a way to retain the nuances of these lighter roast, single origin coffees. Customer preference for roast levels will continue to change. Perfecting coffee tastes will continue to evolve, as will customer curiosity.

Progressive specialty coffee roasters and café owners will continue to explore the reaches of coffee's potential. The day is approaching when the flavored hot coffee drink that has defined the bottom line for the industry will be in serious competition with espresso and slow-brewed single origin coffees with no milk at all. Local barista throw downs and national and worldwide barista and brewer competitions are mobilizing the international coffee community. Being a barista today is a true profession, and can lead to a promising career path.

You and your team are the key elements in sweeping your customers up in enthusiasm for the coffee experience. An engaged customer can easily turn into a return customer, who ultimately takes personal ownership of your brand. The power to evolve with this rapidly maturing industry is in your hands. The deeper you get into the specialty coffee industry, the easier it will be to evolve and adapt to the latest trends.

Congratulations on finishing your first read of this book. Spend today quickly re-reading "today's action" section of each day to burn key takeaways into your mind. As you finish each action day, you are now ready to jot down at least one action idea in the following brand plan note section, as you prepare to write your SBI and business plan.

Once completed, make your wishes a reality within an ambitious time frame. In less than a year, your coffee house can become recognized as the best in your community. Your personal satisfaction and bottom-line profit will underscore that this difficult brand defining journey has been worth the work, heart, and soul you have poured into creating, or dramatically enhancing every customer experience.

Action Day Notes

Day 1: Branding is everything. Everything is Branding.

_____

_____

_____

_____

Day 2: Create a Flexible Brand

_____

_____

_____

_____

Day 3: Be Unique, But Not Odd

_____

_____

_____

_____

Day 4: Learn From Other Industries

_____

_____

_____

_____

Day 5: Differentiate Your Brand

_____

_____

_____

_____

DAY 6: MAKE ALL DECISIONS WITH YOUR CUSTOMER IN MIND

_____

_____

_____

_____

DAY 7: HIRE THE RIGHT EMPLOYEES

_____

_____

_____

_____

DAY 8: YOU HAD ME AT HELLO

_____

_____

_____

_____

DAY 9: STAFF AND SELF-EDUCATION

_____

_____

_____

_____

DAY 10: EDUCATE YOUR CUSTOMERS

_____

_____

_____

_____

Day 11: Keep Expanding Your Barista's Role

_____

_____

_____

_____

Day 12: The Evolution of Barista Basics Training

_____

_____

_____

_____

Day 13: Motivate Your Team

_____

_____

_____

_____

Day 14: Fewer, Better, and Unique Menu Options

_____

_____

_____

_____

Day 15: Be Unique Within Your Category

_____

_____

_____

_____

DAY 16: CAFÉ LAYOUT AND DESIGN

DAY 17: SUSTAINABILITY AND TRANSPARENCY

DAY 18: KEEP IT SOCIAL

DAY 19: COFFEE WITH A CAUSE

DAY 20: CREATE YOUR OWN SPECIFIC BRAND IMAGE (SBI)

Day 21: Navigate with a Plan

_____

_____

_____

_____

Day 22: Owner's Playbook

_____

_____

_____

_____

_____

_____

_____

_____

_____

_____

_____

_____

_____

_____

_____

_____

_____

_____

_____

_____